'Daylight is simply a sup
discursive, funny, restrai.   ..ıg
The Details, I felt as I do at   , great book:
washed clean and scoured c   ..ımade and remade.

'Like all great art, *The Details* is about many things at
once: among them birth and death, laughter and misery,
mothers and children, the body and the spirit – and
informing and transforming all this, of course, it is about
reading and the creation of a sustaining inner life. It
reminds us that in life as in writing, it's the illuminating
detail that reveals the truth of who we are.

'If you love reading, you'll cherish this book
for showing you why.'

CHARLOTTE WOOD

The
Details

Also by Tegan Bennett Daylight

Six Bedrooms
Bombora
What Falls Away
Safety

The
Details

On Love,
Death and
Reading

TEGAN BENNETT DAYLIGHT

SCRIBNER

SCRIBNER

First published in Australia in 2020 by
Scribner, an imprint of Simon & Schuster (Australia) Pty Ltd, 2020
Suite 19A, Level 1, Building C, 450 Miller St, Cammeray, NSW, 2062

Sydney London New York Toronto New Delhi
Visit our website at simonandschuster.com.au

SCRIBNER and design are registered trademarks of The Gale Group, Inc.,
used under licence by Simon & Schuster Inc.

10 9 8 7 6 5 4

  This project has been assisted by the
Commonwealth Government through
the Australia Council, its arts funding
and advisory body.

A Cataloguing-in-Publication entry for this book
is available from the National Library of Australia
9781760855253 (paperback)
9781760855277 (eAudio)
9781760855260 (eBook)

Cover design by Alissa Dinallo
Typeset by Midland Typesetters, Australia
Printed and bound in Australia by Griffin Press

For Russell

Contents

Detail I

When I told my mother I was bored, she would start a pilgrimage around the house. She'd go from room to room, shelf to shelf, and come back with a pile of eight or ten books. She'd sit on the edge of my bed and slide the pile apart, describing each book. Some of them I knew I would never read, either because I'd already tried them and found their first few pages dull, or because the lettering on the cover or the font inside was too small, suggesting a density of thought that I would find impenetrable. But in general every pile contained two or three books I could read, and boredom would be held off for another day or two.

My mother used books as a form of communication. It wasn't simply the exchange I've just described – her giving me books she'd read and loved as a child, and hoping I would love them too – but the words in the books themselves. If we drove towards the Gladesville Bridge at night, the lights of cars cascading down its curve, she would quote Hart Crane, who described headlights in 'The Bridge' as 'the immaculate sigh of stars'. *Hamlet* formed a great deal of her spoken language – if I came home from school after a bad day, she'd sigh about the slings and arrows. If you asked her whether she was telling the truth about something, she was likely to answer, ''Tis true: 'tis true 'tis pity, / And pity 'tis 'tis true.'

Now that I talk in this way to my own children, I know what was happening for her. The words of great writers somehow enrich experience – in borrowing them to describe our own lives we're amplifying what we've seen or felt or heard. In high school I had to study the poetry of Philip Larkin, which – back then – I found mostly a collection of depressing observations about a world that I was thankful had very little to do with my own. But I memorised the single poem I liked, 'Ambulances', and could not – and cannot – see an ambulance without hearing in my head, 'A wild white face that overtops / Red stretcher-blankets momently / As it is carried in and stowed.' When two friends died in a car accident a month or so before our final exams this poem haunted me, troubled me – and somehow informed my imaginings about what had happened that night.

*

Mum – Deborah Bennett – was born Deborah Snowden Trahair in 1941, the fourth and much the youngest child of Alice and Geoff. Alice Snowden and Geoff Trahair married against the wishes of his strictly Methodist family, after meeting at an Australian Communist Party gathering early in the 1930s. Alice was older than Geoff and wore a tennis dress to their wedding – the only white clothing she owned.

I don't know how long into their marriage it was when Geoff's brain tumour was diagnosed, but it was after the births of Nick, Tim and Catherine. I don't even know what kind of brain tumour it was. There are photographs of Geoff with his head half shaved, stitches train-tracking across his skull. He endured several operations and treatment I find hard to imagine – what did they do for brain tumours in the 1940s? Deborah was born after the diagnosis, the surprise child of the marriage. Geoff's illness was always a feature of her life. At some point he took up a course of cold showers as a kind of general health improver. What Mum remembered particularly – and most fondly – was the sound of his screams as he turned the tap on.

She also remembered reading aloud from the Bible on Sunday mornings while the strictly atheist Geoff lay patiently listening in bed. She had conceived a passion for Elsie Dinsmore, the eponymous heroine of a series of books written by American author Martha Finley in the late nineteenth century. Elsie is a little girl so pious that, despite her terror of authority, she stands up to her hot-headed, sinful father when he demands (amongst other things) that she break the Sabbath. His attempts to break her will, and her subsequent 'brain fever', make for compelling reading. The limp, half-dead but still virtuous Elsie became a heroine of mine, too.

Geoff committed suicide late in 1950, when Mum was nine. He had tried before, several times, but Mum didn't know this. When he died she was not told that he had killed himself. On the night after his death the rest of the family – Alice and the four children – were taken to dinner by friends so that Alice would not have to cook. Later, Mum felt guilty about enjoying this so much.

In the year following, Mum developed headaches whose cause no-one could diagnose. Alice, who had been studying for several years in anticipation of Geoff's decline, so that she could find a job to support the five of them, had begun work as a legal secretary. Mum was not well enough – or did not feel well enough – to go to school, and so she spent nearly a year, between the ages of nine and ten, at home on her own.

Later she'd paint pictures of this, which still hang on my father's walls: the view from beds, from floors, the view to be had from someone small sitting next to a door and playing marbles. This is easy for me to imagine – a house empty in the long hours of the day, all its uses quiescent. Clocks tick when you are at home alone, but bedclothes, chairs, cups and saucers on the kitchen bench remain still and noiseless. The sounds of the day come in like a radio turned down in another room. In fact, the radio was Mum's only company. She listened to serials every day. I am not sure what else she did, apart from read.

Amongst the books Mum brought me to read when I was a child were *The Secret Garden* and *A Little Princess*, as well as their author Frances Hodgson Burnett's smash hit, *Little Lord Fauntleroy*. I haven't met an adult my age who has read this book but I did so several times. It's a sticky book, guided by that strange Victorian obsession with 'the little mother' – the same obsession that Virginia Woolf, a child of Victorian parents, grappled with in her diaries and her fiction. Somehow, though, I learned to overlook the archaic, to be open to the oddnesses of different eras, and to read for something else. That something else was what I describe to my students as 'sensory detail'; the minutiae of life that is the real stuff that makes up a book.

I've been teaching writing and literature for a long time, and I hear myself talking about sensory detail a lot. So many of my students write stories bristling with intent, a row of archers, arrows aimed at their 'topic'. They forget that there are such things as weather or food, or 'wild white faces', or headlights on their slow decline over the arch of a bridge in darkness. When I want to explain sensory detail to my students I find myself talking about the Harry Potter series, which I'll confess I don't like much, but they do. I ask them to consider whether it's the lists of richly imagined foods, the all-flavour jellybeans, the butter beer, the pumpkin juice, and the feasts in the Great Hall that are the books' real attraction. It depresses me to think that the appeal might lie in their saccharine hero and his invented difficulties. (His quickly solved problems always remind me of the Flight of the Conchords' song that satirises *Lord of the Rings*: 'We'll never make it – there's thousands of them and only nine of us [pause]. We made it!') Too many of my students tell me that Harry's adventures teach them that however hard things are, they can always overcome their problems – to which I want to say, 'Tell that to Anne Frank' – but just enough of them seem to wake up when I mention the food in Harry Potter. Like Edmund's Turkish delight or Mr and Mrs Beaver's freshly caught and cooked fish in *The Lion, the Witch and the Wardrobe*, the butter beer and the all-you-can-eat-of-whatever-you-want feasts speak directly to something very simple in humans. Sensory detail: food as comfort, as reward, as enchantment; a sled riding crisply over white snow; the smell of earth in a garden that has just been weeded.

For me, detail yields metaphor, the most useful tool of the writing teacher. I think of *The Secret Garden* almost every time I teach. I hear myself saying to students, 'Let that word breathe – take all the other words out from around it.' And when I'm saying it, I'm thinking of Mary using a stick to dig between the green shoots in the walled garden in her freezing, unfriendly new home. When I teach writing or literature I feel as though I am the owner of a storehouse or a granary that floats in the air behind me. All those books, all of that detail, just waiting to be called on. And when I say 'granary' and 'floats' in the same sentence, I know I am somehow referring to, or calling up, Keats' spirit of autumn, sitting 'careless on a granary floor, / . . . hair soft-lifted by the winnowing wind'. I turn to look into my storehouse and there is Mary kneeling in the earth, making space between the newly shot bulbs, and I know straight away that this is an image about writing; that Frances Hodgson Burnett, whether she knew it or not, was writing about writing, and waiting for me to call her back into being.

When Mum was dying we three grown children spent as much time with her as we could, taking turns to drive to Sydney from the Blue Mountains. She liked having us on the bed with her. Any of us – my sister knitting, my brother reading aloud. One of her six grandchildren, legs under the covers, reading a book or sharing the crossword with her. Mum spent three weeks in hospital, just a few months before she died, and I would come and squeeze onto the single bed with her and read to her. In that season of painless dying, when her suffering was suspended in a sort of autumnal kindness, mediated by the soft movement of nurses around her and the knowledge that any crisis, big or small, would be somehow managed by others, we reread Gerald Durrell's *My Family and Other Animals*.

My Family and Other Animals has more sensory detail than any other book I have read. Without having a copy near me I can call up Lugaretzia, the moaning maid with bowel problems, whose physician, as Larry Durrell says, will need 'a pick and a miner's lamp'. I can remember ripe grapes held to the mouth and squeezed for their contents, their leathery skins discarded. I can remember the battle, on Gerry's walls and ceiling, between Cicely the giant praying mantis and Geronimo the gecko, and the bloodied scratches on Geronimo's skin after he has defeated her. I can remember Theo running up the stairs, followed by the whole family, to watch the seaplane landing, its wake arrowed behind it on a bright blue Aegean.

Mum turned to her own storehouse of detail to speak about what was happening. She was *worried* about dying. I can't put it more clearly than that. She didn't really believe in an afterlife but she was troubled by the thought of not returning. Back at home, in the weeks when we were trying to set up the second bedroom as a comfortable place to die, we talked about it, and she used Hamlet's words to describe what might lie ahead: 'the undiscover'd country, from whose bourn no traveller returns'. I don't think she believed that she would never return. I don't think I believed it either. I was busy being very capable, and critical of others who wept at my mother's bedside, because part of me thought that I would have my chance to cry later. When all this was over. When I could speak to Mum alone. When I could tell her that it felt as though she was alive in me, and that if she died it might do some grievous damage to who I was.

She dreamed, in those last months, that she was on a beach and three figures rose out of the water and walked up the shore towards her. They were her father, her mother, and her sister Catherine, who had died more than fifteen years earlier. She didn't describe the beach to me.

I didn't read the Australian classic *Pioneer Shack* by Dora Birtles, although I've still got Mum's copy – it was the book she read most in childhood, the book she inhabited. A few years ago I was on stage at a writers' festival with the Australian author Joan London. Imagine a shyer, more softly spoken Chrissy Amphlett, and you have Joan: slender, with dyed black hair and an ageing and beautiful face, she dresses like a rock star and speaks hesitantly, with a refined Australian accent and much ducking of her head to look embarrassedly into her lap. I asked her if she could remember the books that had haunted her childhood, and she looked startled, as she had at most questions. She said, 'There was a book, a book about children who built their own house. But I can't remember what it was called. I loved it. I read it over and over.'

I said, also hesitantly, '*Pioneer Shack?*'

'That's it!'

Mum had been dead more than a year by this time. But as Joan was talking about *Pioneer Shack*, there it was, that conversation with Mum, which had been so continuous, so constant in my life that the book was just below the surface of my conscious mind. It was easy to retrieve.

It wasn't only the sensory detail in books that caught Mum's magpie attention. She was what the critic James Wood might call 'a serious noticer'. Before she died, I hadn't known that she'd taught me to notice, because she hadn't exactly taught me. She'd just noticed, but done it out loud; she was always pointing things out to us. Young currawongs, the feathers on their rumps still fluffy and grey, as though

they wore nappies. A dog in Wentworth Falls who had an expression just like James Dean's. I didn't believe this until I saw it. The dog – a border collie – had a kind of set to its jaw and narrowed eyes. It lay with its paws crossed on the nature strip outside its house and watched you insolently as you walked by. Just like James Dean.

In the days after Mum's death all this became apparent to me. I felt as though I could suddenly recognise the parts of myself, as though I was being put together, made, like a toy you had to assemble. Parts of me clicking into place. I knew then, without having ever considered it, that somehow my mother had communicated her vivid vision of life to me. That I had learned to see by seeing alongside her. I also began to realise that the perfect parent for a writer is the almost-writer, the person or persons trembling on the brink of self-expression. Someone as full of words as my mother – and indeed my father – must inevitably spill them into their offspring.

Of course I now collect piles of books for my own children when they say they are bored. I keep trying them with my old copy of Ernest Thompson Seton's *Two Little Savages*, a nineteenth-century novel drawing on the author's Canadian childhood – his cruel, critical and exacting father, and the boy's longing for an escape into nature.

The character based on Thompson Seton, Yan, is shyly passionate about the natural world and wishes most of all to be Native American, to let the woods be his only source of shelter and food. Yan becomes sick – from lack of love, the book seems to imply – and is sent to live on a farm. There the father is just as exacting but kinder. Yan forms a real friendship with Sam Raften, the oldest son of the family, and together they venture further and further into the woods. Finally Mr Raften gives them permission to spend a month there, alone. They build a wigwam. They make arrows and quivers. They shoot birds and catch fish, they make fires, they try to dance, and make themselves sick smoking pipes.

I suppose *Two Little Savages* is my *Pioneer Shack* – the story of children who somehow strike out on their own, make their own dwelling, find their own food. It was the most attractive story you could have told a child like me, a child whose life was like a dinghy always tied to the jetty. We three children read Frances Hodgson Burnett, *Swallows and Amazons*, the Narnia books, all of Tintin and much of the Famous Five. All those deserted, orphaned or fortuitously parentless children of nineteenth- and twentieth-century fiction feeding themselves, building shelters, in a way their readers never had to. And all that detail – all that food and weather, water and light.

How strange it is to be one of the carriers of my mother's detail: the silent hours alone in the house in Gladesville, the sound of her father shrieking in the shower, the three familiar figures rising to greet her on the beach. When I read, I am still in conversation with her. All that detail sings in the air, living still.

Vagina

1.

Every ten years or so in a reading life, a book comes along that makes us think, Oh! This can be *said*! And, if we are writers, or interested in the art of writing, Oh! This can be *done*! I probably first had this experience with Helen Garner's *Monkey Grip*. Later, with Toni Morrison's *Beloved*. Later still, with Kazuo Ishiguro's *The Remains of the Day*. Most latterly, with Karl Ove Knausgaard's 'My Struggle' series. I couldn't believe a writer could simply pile up experience the way Knausgaard did, and make it interesting. He seemed to leave nothing out.

But literature always leaves things out; it can't ever tell the whole story, or even half of it. When you write you find yourself inventing characters without friends, or with families who are dead or just far away; you exclude neighbourhoods, fashions, technology; or, like Jane Austen, you ignore wars and slavery and work. You can't contain the multitudes of life. Even Knausgaard can't record every piss or shit, every phone call, every exchange with a friend. Literature looks for significances; it yearns towards composition – order – and in so doing has sometimes to pretend that people, bodily functions, political movements, injustices simply aren't there.

It is the same with our bodies; most of the time we have to ignore the narrative of the foot, the ear or the arse. There is a brief period when a baby begins to apprehend its body; I remember both my daughter and son holding their hands in front of them as they lay in their cots, turning them this way and that, examining them. Here is something that belongs to me – if I do *this*, it moves. But this soon disappears into the deep, oblivious happiness of the healthy. Like literature, we have to move forward.

A vagina is a thing we sometimes notice, partly because we are told to notice it, early on. It distinguishes us from our brothers. It becomes a source of pleasure. It is an entrance to our body. But until it became an exit I didn't consider it closely.

My two labours were relatively uncomplicated, and successful – the first involved some intervention with scissors and drugs; the second lasted ninety minutes, leaving no time for intervention of any sort. Both babies were well. My husband helped me and held onto me throughout, and we both cried a lot at the end.

My first child was my daughter, Alice, who is now eighteen. The labour of bringing Alice out took eleven or twelve hours, beginning with a pain that I could hold at bay as long as I was standing up. I spent a full day on my feet, walking around and around the old motor raceway near our house, washing dishes, folding clothes, watching TV with Russell, him in the blue armchair, me standing behind him.

As soon as I reached the point at which the pain stayed whether I was upright or not, all I wanted was to go back, to not have a baby, to have never been pregnant. But there is nothing so inexorable as birth, unless it is death. My husband drove me to the hospital and delivered me to the back entrance, the special place for labouring mothers. I remember that I started taking my clothes off as I was being led through the doors. I was so hot. No-one said anything.

It was a straightforward labour, and in four or five hours my cervix was fully dilated – ready for the exit of a baby. Almost ready. There are stages, and it seemed to me that I was in the final one.

But I didn't know – although I'd been told – what the final stage of labour was meant to feel like. Like loss, labour makes no sense until it is experienced. Throughout the previous months I'd felt like an athlete training for an event

I had no real picture of, an event that might take place in the sea or on land or in space. And because I was fully dilated and already so sick of the labour and so desperate for it to be over, and because I thought that fully dilated meant ready, I asked the midwife if I could push. She said yes. So I began. I leaned against the wall and pushed – tried to force the baby out of myself. I leaned against my husband and pushed. I leaned against the bed and pushed. Push and return, push and return. This was what it felt like: every time I pushed I had the sense of Alice coming down – and then of her being pulled back into my body as soon as I relaxed. This went on for three hours.

I do wish I'd known that I wasn't ready to push, and I wish the midwife had known for me. But I'd never had a labour before; the experience was not what I'd read about or imagined, and it moved too quickly for me to adapt my training to it. And she wasn't a perfect midwife. A perfect midwife recognises everything, I suppose: she becomes one with the labouring mother, and can help her find the moment when she is ready for this or for that. It's an art, and not everyone has the gift. This midwife was possibly as sick of the whole thing as I was, and she was not gifted.

In my second labour, with my son, Patrick, the final stage announced itself very clearly. This is the story I'm going to tell my daughter when it is her turn. I'll say, The final stage feels like expulsion. The body makes the decisions, not you. Think of heaving when vomiting, the way the body takes over and hurls out whatever your stomach can't retain. It is wholly involuntary. This is what a real final stage feels like, or at least it does for me. Your body heaves and contracts and forces and throws out the baby. The midwife at Patrick's birth – a luckier one, or a better one – saw, and said it was time. Three pushes – a baby.

I have a friend whose grandmother went into her first labour without having had it explained to her that the baby would come out of her vagina. She was from the north of England, working class, Catholic – and it was the 1950s. I laughed in horror and amazement when I was first told this. Imagine not knowing.

But it didn't make any difference to know, as it turned out. You can see as many pictures as you like of a baby sliding down that *birth canal*, but those last hours of your first labour seem to have nothing to do with it. You don't think about your vagina, but if you did you might just think, No. This cannot happen. You think instead of caesareans, of tearings open, of your stomach bursting and you dying as it does so, in a great explosion of relief. All those books I'd read in which women died in childbirth returned to me afterwards and I felt as though I had to mourn the hordes of them who had, and still were. I have seen deaths. But I can't think of a worse one.

In the first labour I finally crawled onto the bed and lay there asking for an epidural. Every time a contraction came I wept and curled up. I think my body by now was entering the final stage of labour – I do remember the beginnings of that throwing-up feeling, the uncontrollable heaving – but I didn't want to know about it. I'm still sorry I wasn't up to it.

It took a while for the anaesthetist to come, because we live in a regional area and he had to travel. The injection he gave me in my spine cleared the pain of the contractions completely. It was exactly like waking from a nightmare. I sat up, I could see; the room became a room instead of a looming cave of hell. I could hear properly. I could see Russell. I would be able to deliver the baby now.

But it was evident that something hadn't progressed in the way that it should have, and I would need help. I could hardly push now – I was exhausted, and I could not recognise, thank god, the feeling of a contraction, which is what you are meant to push with, or against. The obstetrician, also from out of town, preferred forceps to the ventouse (the rubber suction cup placed over the baby's head that is more commonly used now). For a few minutes I had been safe, but as he came towards me with the forceps – servers for a terrible salad – I could feel myself going back into the cave of hell. I remember him sliding them one handle at a time into my vagina. Not sliding, not inserting: manoeuvring, angling, pushing. This was the moment I understood that the epidural had removed the sensation of contractions but nothing else. I could feel my vagina.

Forceps in, he quickly reached behind him for something else. Scissors.

Russell says he thought, Tegan's not going to like this. He thought it because an episiotomy was the thing we were all told to avoid. Enough reading and conversation tells you that an episiotomy – cutting the vagina down towards the anus to make a wider opening for the baby – is not a good thing. It's not necessary, say the books and conversation, because if the vagina needs to tear it will tear 'naturally' (before giving birth you ignore words like these – you think you are listening but you're not). A surgical cut won't heal as well, it may cause problems with continence, it may start a bigger, worse tear than would have happened of its own accord.

Russell was right, I didn't like it, but it had nothing to do with my 'plan' for the birth, which was not rigid, only hopeful. I did not like it because I could feel it. It takes strength and skill and guts to cut through flesh when someone is scream-ing, but that's what the obstetrician did, and out came Alice. They had to give my vagina many small injections of local anaesthetic before they could stitch me up.

Afterwards, when my sister was carrying Alice around the room and singing to her, and Russell and I were holding hands and wiping our tears, one of the midwives gave me a shot of pethidine. 'We usually only do this for caesars,' was what she said. So on that first night the pain was not too great.

After that, the pain was quite – painful. I walked very little for those five days I was in hospital, but it was deeply uncomfortable sitting up to breastfeed, with my whole weight on the site of my wound. I wasn't allowed any more pethidine but I was given Panadeine Forte, and many condoms that had been filled with water and frozen. You lay these along the thick maternity pad that you already have in your pants to soak up the rivers of blood that you pass after giving birth. They cool the sore vagina, and ease the pain a bit. Pretty quickly the heat of your vagina and blood melts these ice penises, so you peel them out, along with the maternity pad and all the blood, and start again.

But breastfeeding was causing me fresh pain. The first couple of times were fine. By the third time – and Alice was feeding every two or three hours – I was developing blisters on my nipples. Her small mouth and its ridgy gums felt like an oyster closing over my breast. I loved feeding her because she needed it so much, and my breasts were so full of colostrum that I was desperate to empty them, so hard with milk that you could have knocked on them like a door; just to touch them brought exquisite agony. But it was difficult to keep feeding because every time I did the blisters grew worse – and there would be that oystery little mouth again, clamping down on them.

So although it hurt, I couldn't pay a great deal of attention to my vagina. I only thought about it when I was on my feet. When I stood up to go to the toilet or change Alice's nappy I shuffled, wide-legged, like a hurt cowboy.

I also knew I had to open my bowels at some point. But I was avoiding it. Avoiding voiding. When I sat on the toilet

I had to look up at the ceiling and chant just to urinate. The piss ran over the wound and it hurt a lot. If I put my fingers down I could feel the bristle of stitches, like little wires in my vagina. If I pushed at all – and I made a gentle effort to do so – they bulged, and the pain was very great. So I didn't try.

I had a room of my own, a luxury few of my city friends had; you need private health insurance or a stroke of weird luck to secure a single room in a Sydney hospital. It was midwinter in the mountains but my room faced north and was full of a gentle sunlight, and the days, despite the pain, were loving and warm. Sometimes at night I thought that if I'd had injuries like this from anything but birth there would have been ambulances, police, counselling. If I'd hurt myself this way in a car accident there would have been weeks put aside for recovery and rehabilitation. Instead I was sleeping only a few hours a night and I was about to step back into a life that was utterly changed.

But during the days, when time flowed past me like a stream, dipping and changing in the sun, I also thought, This is the happiest I have ever been: Alice wrapped in her cotton blanket and serene beside me, and the life of the hospital quietly passing by our door. I loved her, and still love her, overwhelmingly. What an interesting feeling it was – animal, but separable into parts. Part of my love was pride.

*

We left hospital on a Tuesday. Coming out into the winter morning with the baby in my arms was shocking. The noise of the highway was like a howl. It was so cold and the light hurt our eyes; Alice winced and started crying. I was dizzy and my stitches were hurting. Levering my screaming newborn into the car, all I could think was that I was entrusting that fragile head to a kind of missile. It felt impossible that we would drive out into the traffic with her. It felt as though she had nothing to protect her.

We pulled up at the back of our house, which was a communal area for all the cottages in our street. Russell took the baby in her capsule and my bag and strode inside, and all I had to do was walk across the shared space, through the gate, and across the grass to our open back door. But as soon as I got out of the car something was very wrong: the pain in my vagina was much worse; there was a pressure, a bursting feeling, and then a terrible rush in my pants. I couldn't run but I got as quickly as possible to the bathroom, closed the door, pulled down my pants and sat, and another rush of shit went where it was meant to go. Tears ran down my face. I could hear Alice screaming in Russell's arms. I had to have a shower to clean myself.

I'd already given a name to the phenomenon of hearing your baby screaming when you shower, even if she isn't screaming: I called it Ghost Babies. Every new parent gets Ghost Babies in the shower, because the running water has a pitch that sounds like a baby's scream. This wasn't Ghost

Babies, though; Alice screamed the whole way through. When your first baby screams it makes you frantic, so I showered as quickly as possible.

However, my vagina healed very well, and I didn't have any more accidents like that one.

Enough has been said by others about the first weeks with a new baby. Part of the shock was that I was not allowed to rest. Instead of the weeks of rehabilitation I was on my feet more than I'd ever been in my life. It was the start of never sitting down, a period that runs right through parenting life but is at its peak when children are very young. My feet ached. My healing vagina also ached.

Sometimes I put my fingers in my pants and then smelt them. They were – pissy. Pissier than usual. I wasn't doing any running, so I wasn't having the sudden leakages friends and my sister had described. I was starting to do my pelvic floor exercises because I was going to a weekly mothers' meeting run by a midwife who brightly described them to us as 'going up like a lift!' 'One floor,' she said, grimacing lightly, 'the next floor' – grimacing a little more – 'and the third floor' – big grimace. 'Hold and – release!' I couldn't do them very well – on certain days it felt as though I couldn't even feel my pelvic floor muscles. But I tried, and things were okay.

And this is just one birth. Eight months later one of my friends laboured without pain relief for thirty-eight hours. When the birth-centre midwife stitched her vagina after it tore, it was so swollen that she stitched it wrongly, joined parts that should not be joined, caused a new vaginal entrance that was not natural. After this my friend could not have sex, wear a tampon, even put a finger inside her vagina.

2.

In my late teens and early twenties I could read away entire days, get up from a bed damp with the print of my body feeling utterly disoriented, as though I lived in the book. Voices took me over, colonised me; I had problems distinguishing myself from the likes of Zooey Glass, and Nora in *Monkey Grip*.

I had less time for reading once Alice was born. Russell used to call what I did *breastreading*; as I was settling Alice down to feed I'd be groping around for my book. I used to prop it on her stomach. Best to read small, old books in this situation – my copies of *Barchester Towers* and *Middlemarch* had soft leather covers and stayed obediently open as they rested against the baby. I couldn't, later, do this with my son, who would empty a breast in three minutes – before I could get myself properly lodged inside a sentence. Alice fed slowly and dreamily.

These old books were about religion, love, landscape. There would always be childbirth, and deaths in childbirth – but never on stage. Always hidden.

*

When Alice was eight months old my period started again. It had been nice not to think about that. We'd been careful not to get pregnant, though; we knew I could be fertile only weeks after the birth. We had friends who'd been fooled, friends with babies twelve or fourteen months apart. But we knew our limits. My period started and it became clear that I could no longer use tampons. 'I just sort of . . . walk them out,' said my sister, and that was exactly my experience. A tampon went in okay but as I left the bathroom it would start to corkscrew out of me. I turned to pads. I am wearing one now. I can feel the blood as it leaves me – a little pump, a flush into the pad.

It's hard to recall those days in detail, though detail was all there was. But life with children rushes on, and every day you're reinventing yourself, every day responding to something you've never seen before. I'm trying to slow down, to remember, be honest about the change in the landscape, which was as though a glacier gave up inching down a mountain and decided to get it over and done with in a day. *Whoosh*. Landscape changed.

I've said that the birth of my son was straightforward, which it was. Both my births began with my waters breaking (for most women, this happens during labour). With Alice, it happened twenty-four hours before she was born. With Paddy, perhaps six hours. Some time after my waters broke (a little feeling of pressure, a shove from the baby, and pop – our bed was soaked), the labour began. No gentle lead-up,

27

no mild pains as with Alice. I was suddenly in full labour; I was suddenly in the bath, head down and chanting; I was suddenly at the hospital and the perfect midwife was saying, 'This baby's coming! I'm going to prep!'

I needed to be down low, so Russell quickly found himself a place on the soft armchair in the labour ward and reached out for me. I fell onto my knees in front of him, and slammed my elbows into his thighs. I put my face in his lap. And with every contraction I rammed my head as hard as I could into his chest. I can still remember the feel and smell of his flannelette shirt, and forcing him backwards as hard as I could, and him resisting, keeping still for me, his muscles quivering. Three of these, four of these. The midwife was behind me, ready to catch the baby, helping me to stay calm, saying, 'Tegan, try to be quiet so you can hear me telling you when to push,' in a kind and comforting voice. I must have been screaming. I didn't explode – but as with the first birth, I thought I might, and even hoped I might. And Patrick was born.

I had a small tear, a natural tear, and I wept as it was stitched up because of the last time. I was frightened of having needles and scissors near my vagina. But it wasn't too bad. I knew how to breastfeed this time and Paddy latched on straight away, and we were taken to our room, and Russell went home to get Alice, and all was well. Our children had been born in the same room, in the same hospital, at the same time of day.

*

I began to notice a problem when Paddy was a year or so old. He was a big baby, who walked quite late, like his sister, so he was often in my arms. And if I'd thought I didn't get much rest with the first baby – well, this was a new situation altogether. When Alice was a baby and had daytime naps, I'd tried to use one of them to sleep myself. But when Paddy had naps, Russell needed a break and that was when Alice needed me. I lay on the bed and read books to her. Sometimes I'd wake with the book still held above my head and Alice saying, 'Mum. Mum. Mum.'

The problem was a bulge in my vagina. It didn't hurt. But it felt odd, and uncomfortable, because it kept reminding me that I had a vagina, when I didn't want to think about it. It felt as though someone had inserted a small balloon in there, about the size of a plum. I could put my fingers in and push it back up, but it always came back down again.

I didn't tell many people about it because I was starting to feel ashamed. It was difficult to talk about. I mentioned it to a friend, who said that she'd fixed her 'problem' – unidentified – with yoga and running. This silenced me quickly. I had no time for yoga. No inclination to go running. The best thing I could do for sore muscles and an inflexible body was to pour a glass of wine or have a beer. I had a strict rule – I could drink between the hours of five and seven pm, but not before or after. I broke this once and poured a glass of white at three pm, when both children were screaming.

When I tell my friends without children these stories they always wince, as I would too. But it's hard to explain how major – and minor – these vaginal events have been. If I'd been told as a 25-year-old what could happen to my vagina, I might have resisted it. I might have decided not to have children. Although the chances are I would have thought what I first thought when I was 'educated' about these things during pregnancy – something along the lines of *Never gonna happen.*

In a letter to her sister, Cassandra, Jane Austen called one of their sisters-in-law (after an eleventh or twelfth lying-in) a 'poor animal'. After two children my vagina seemed not to be doing its job. But what might have happened if I'd had six, or seven, or twelve or thirteen babies? What if I was one of the poor animals that Austen helped to care for after each birth? How did they hide from her that their vaginas might be hurting, or leaking, or bulging? Or did she know, and keep it quiet?

I thought of Edward Lear, who was the sixteenth of seventeen children. I thought of Edward Lear's mother, who left his upbringing to his sisters, but probably didn't just faint on the sofa after his birth, because there would have been toddlers, five-year-olds, ten-year-olds for her to take care of. What had happened to her vagina? Was it still robust after all those babies? Could she piss or shit successfully? Was there anyone she could talk to about it?

Of course literature generally pretends that the vagina isn't there, unless it's juxtaposed with a penis. The characters

30

are thinking about their marriages, or the deaths of friends or children or parents, or about war, or money. I don't think I've seen any of them sneaking off to bathrooms to push their fingers up their vaginas to relieve the pressure of a prolapsed bowel or rectum. Is this literature anyway? It might be, if I were Knausgaard. Imagine if I wrote the details of my life. Months, years of vaginas and vagina-related thoughts. Would you read it?

Knausgaard tells us that the idea of fiction collapsed for him, that 'the only genres I saw value in, that still conferred meaning, were diaries and essays, the types of literature that did not deal with narrative . . .' But set pen to paper and narrative exists. Maths textbooks, laundry lists – stories all. Even Knausgaard's writing, diffuse as it may seem, is a way of taking control. What a relief writing is.

My vaginal issues were starting to make me feel as though I was losing control of the narrative of my own life. I could not talk to anyone about this except Russell; I could not make a story out of it. I wonder if other women, other readers, have felt this way.

Alice started school, and her school was a five-minute walk from our house, but you had to cross the Great Western Highway to reach it. I'd push the pram with Paddy in it up our street, cross at the crossing – and then we had to climb sixty or so steps to the bridge. It was always fun, with mothers and fathers and children catching up on the bridge, talking, skipping, waving to the trucks to get them to honk their horns.

At first I'd turn around as we started up the stairs and pull the pram up with Paddy in it. But this was slow, and before long the pram started to come apart from the crashing on each step. It was easier to carry him, and he liked it too. It wasn't always my day to go to school; Russell and I took turns. But a couple of days a week I would carry Paddy up the steps and over the bridge, and back again.

I've said he was a big baby; he was dense with the kind of muscle that Alice had never seemed to have. He was heavy. And nobody had said to me – or I hadn't heard – that carrying heavy weights was the worst thing for your pelvic floor. I carried him up and down the steps, across the bridge, and all around the house, and the bulge in my vagina got worse. It was making me feel embarrassed – but worse, frustrated. I felt stupid. I had a stupid vagina. I told Russell about it. Russell persuaded me to go to the GP, and the GP found me a pelvic floor physiotherapist.

The physio was in her early sixties. She was small and neat and practical, with blonde hair that was greying prettily. She had me lie down on her special bed with my underpants off and a paper apron covering my lap, so that when she had to touch my vagina she slid her hand under the apron. Part of the touching involved two fingers thrusting and pushing inside and the physio looking into the middle distance, like a writer trying to think of the end to a story. The walls of my vagina felt unpleasantly elastic under the vigorous shoving of her fingers; this way, that way, it all seemed to give.

Then she got out a penis-shaped probe attached to a sort of meter by a ringed cord, like the one on the receiver of an old telephone. On went the condom, on went the lube, in went the penis. She looked at the meter. 'Cough,' she said. 'Now contract your pelvic muscles. Hold.' I did. We went through this a few times and she tapped in some numbers, and then turned away while I slid the paper apron off me, wiped off the lube and put on my pants.

When I turned back she was holding a sheaf of papers with hand-drawn illustrations of different pelvic floor exercises. She showed me how to do them, told me how often to do them, told me my pelvic floor muscles were weak. She said, 'Your two births have put great strain on your pelvic floor. The long second stage of the first, the quick delivery of the second.' This went a long way towards explaining things; no-one had ever said this to me before. She told me that the little balloon in my vagina was my bladder; I had a partial prolapse. I should be able to sort that out quite quickly. She told me I had to stop carrying heavy things, which would be interesting. I went home with my exercises and hoped for the best.

Things improved a bit but not a lot. I did manage to get rid of the little balloon, but it came back so easily – if I carried anything heavy, like a toddler, or if I sneezed.

Russell carried all the shopping, and Paddy learned to walk up the steps. I kept going back to the physio but the story didn't change. Once, she was showing me something on her screen and accidentally flicked to a client list. I'm a quick reader; in the half a second before she minimised the screen I read the names of several well-known women. That was one of my more comforting visits.

But a year or more later – by this time Paddy was at school too, and I was taking on more work – I got sick. It started with a sore chest. My chest ached. Interestingly ached. Hotly ached. This developed into a kind of flu during which I blew my nose so many times that it blistered. But then it became pneumonia, and of course I coughed. I coughed for weeks – for more than a month. I coughed so much that I tore a muscle in my stomach and had to hold a hand over it when the next cough came. I coughed during an interview on stage and had to leave. I coughed while teaching, I coughed in bed, I coughed if I walked or sat or had a shower. All this coughing put an extra strain on my pelvic floor muscles and in the end I was wetting myself if I did anything sudden. Like cough. The little balloon made itself known again. And my vagina was starting to feel . . . odd.

You'll notice I haven't said much about sex in all of this. It is essential to this story, but the hardest thing to write about. Sex is important. It's fun. It helps us sleep. It brings us and keeps us together. But because of sex we had to talk a lot about my failing vagina, and it took me a long time to manage to do this. I was so ashamed. If the subject came up I was angry. I wanted to ignore it; it couldn't be fixed, so why talk about it? But every time we had sex I was reminded of how elastic – or, let's say it, loose – my vagina had become. This made me furiously resentful. It was Russell who kept encouraging me to talk, staying calm when I got angry, listening, suggesting, considering.

Out in the world it was still hard to talk about it, although I tried a couple of times. Other women were always sympathetic, but it was rare to find anyone offering their own story. Only my friend whose vagina had been stitched wrongly could talk about it. She'd had an operation a year or so after her baby's birth to reshape her vagina, to remake it into its old self. It was successful, and she went on to have two more babies, born at home without problems.

3.

There are three formidable women in my life who all look alike – so alike they could be sisters. These are my agent, my children's Year 3 and 4 teacher, and the gynaecologist I was eventually referred to. They all have the same attractive lion-like quality – a mixture of power, rage and kindness.

The gynaecologist had rooms at the top of a private hospital. She wore a short skirt and high heels; she was heavy-breasted and blonde and not very tall. She stalked around the room talking to me about books and children and my vagina as she found gloves, a gown for me, a lamp to shine between my legs. She put her two fingers in and pushed around, assuming briefly the writer's middle-distance look as she thought about what was going on in there.

Afterwards we sat at her desk and she drew me some pictures. She talked about surgery. And then she said, 'Think of a swimming costume. A stretched swimming costume.' I thought of a swimming costume.

'Once it's stretched,' the gynaecologist went on, 'you can't fix it. It doesn't return to its original elasticity. This is what has happened to your vagina. You can do all the pelvic floor exercises you like for the muscles surrounding it – and you should, they'll support it – but you can't change what's happened to it.'

It was like when the physio told me the births had caused my problems. Finally, the narrative was beginning to make sense. All it took was a metaphor.

'Look,' said the gynaecologist, leaning over her paper again. 'What we need to do is actually remove part of it. See? Make an incision here. Cut some out. Bring the two new edges together.'

I went home and told Russell about it. We decided to leave it, to see if my vagina improved. It didn't. I went back a second time; and the third time, we went together. The gynaecologist said she'd just discovered that the free surgery list at her hospital was being cancelled. 'Health cuts,' she said. She had seven appointments left. 'You need to choose soon,' she said. We couldn't afford to pay for her privately.

We left, caught a bus into the city, had lunch, talked about it some more, and rang her back. 'I've still got a space in June,' she said. So we took it.

I'm left with a vagina that works much better. I still don't run; if I do it leaks. I wear a pad when we play soccer with my brother and sister and nieces and nephews, and I've discovered that my sister does the same when she plays netball.

I have another new problem, and I've given it a name: the Squawking Vagina. I've got time for yoga now and I love it. I need it. But in certain poses – half moon, sometimes downward dog – the two walls of my vagina come together and pull apart with a noise somewhere between a belch and a fart. I was horribly embarrassed the first time this happened at yoga. I said, 'Sorry,' as casually as I could and tried to get on with it, but tears of shame and rage were sliding down my face, and it took me weeks to go back.

When I did, the class was small: three other women and a man. Not the usual kind of ropy tense bald man who goes to yoga. This one was a small Scotsman who was a bit overweight and terrible at yoga. Couldn't touch his toes.

We started our poses. I could feel the Squawking Vagina about to happen – it was another of those mornings – so I straightened up and, blushing and blushing and blushing, said, 'I'm sorry. I've got this problem. I need to explain it.'

Our teacher paused, did her thing of smiling openly, generously. I've always been pretty snooty about the idea of just letting my feelings out, letting the tears flow, and so on. I was grateful for it at that moment.

I told them about the operation as quickly as I could, and the new issue. One of the women looked at her feet, smiling nervously. The Scotsman also blushed, and stayed quiet. The youngest, a woman who looked to be in her thirties, said, 'It happens for me during sex.'

For me too, sometimes, I said (how difficult this was to admit to, even after my first confession – listen to that qualifying 'sometimes'!). We compared notes: how many children we'd had, whether or not the problem improved with time. And the third, a pleasant-faced, ordinary-bodied fifty-something woman who'd always been friendly but whose name I didn't know, said, 'I wear a tampon. That does the trick.'

The next time I went to yoga I put a tampon in. Since the surgery I've been able to wear them again; I don't 'walk them out' anymore. I did half moon. I did downward dog. Not a squawk came out of me. Telling the story made a difference.

I am three-quarters of the way through my first reading of Halldór Laxness's masterwork, *Independent People*. The other day Russell said to me, 'I've never seen you read a book so slowly.' It's true – I am finding it hard to get through, partly because of how deeply I feel when I read it. I've tried to describe some of the scenes to Russell and have to stop for tears. After all these years, I'm still inhabited by books, still colonised by them, still taken over. It's hurt me to read about Bjartur Jónsson's neglected children and wives, their starved lives at the edge of the glacier as he pursues his goal of total independence from others.

Bjartur's first wife dies alone in childbirth while he roams the hills for days, looking for a lost sheep. And it's Bjartur we stay with, following him through the unspeakable cold, compelled by his reckless, stupid bravery. He tries to capture a reindeer and, leaping on its back, is dragged by it into the freezing Glacier River. He survives this, and at last finds his way to a lonely farm not unlike his own, 'roll[ing] in through the doorway armoured from head to foot in ice'.

Meanwhile his wife is dying: labouring, cutting the cord, bleeding. All on her own, and unseen, by writer or reader.

James Wood says, 'To notice is to rescue, to redeem; to save life from itself.' I don't need you to know about my vagina. But I need my literature to know about it. To know women's lives – to know their bodies, and not just words like 'suffering' or 'pain'. The story is still not told, on the page, or between women themselves. The detail is missing, and detail is all there is.

Helen Garner

It is a common misperception about writers (sometimes held by writers themselves) that their experience shapes their writing – as in the case of William Burroughs, who claimed he became a writer the minute he accidentally shot his wife dead in a drunken game of William Tell. Experience may give rise to plot, and it certainly gives rise to emotion, or opinion, but I am in agreement with something once said by Annie Dillard: 'Only after the writer lets literature shape her can she perhaps shape literature.' Writing fiction is a response to reading fiction – it is an answer, an attempt to be part of a conversation. As a six-year-old, I wrote to the author of *The Wombles*, Elisabeth Beresford, and suggested some new plots to her.

Even then it was not enough for me to simply read. I had to join in.

I first began my conversation with Helen Garner's work at fourteen or fifteen, when I found a copy of *Monkey Grip* on my parents' bookshelves. My mother later told me that her friends were shocked she had let me read something with such vivid sex scenes in it. I don't know what to say to this; it seems so stupid. I don't want to paint my mother as a heroine fighting the good fight against the forces of wowserism, of censorship. She just calmly believed what I believe – that literature is a stepping stone towards life. The more you read, the further you get.

In any case it was not the sex that I found arresting in *Monkey Grip*. It was the detail.

Monkey Grip, which was published in 1977, is Garner's first book in a list of closely autobiographical fiction and non-fiction. It tells the story of Nora and Javo. Nora is a woman in her thirties who is living in a succession of shared households in inner-city Melbourne with her young daughter, Gracie. Her life has a constantly changing shape. She has no single job (rather a series of hazy freelance writing jobs) nor anywhere she must be. She shares the care of Gracie with other mothers – and, occasionally, fathers – with whom she lives. She takes drugs. She has sex with many different men, but she is finally and hopelessly in love with Javo, another middle-class white Australian, but this time a junkie. His addiction spells disaster for their attachment, though disaster never quite, or never completely, arrives. *Monkey Grip* keeps us in the same limbo experienced by its narrator. Just when we think we have seen the last of Javo he appears again. He comes to tell Nora that he loves her or that he doesn't; he comes to borrow money for drugs, or to swear that he will never use drugs again. He surges and recedes, surges and recedes.

I hadn't read such unstructured fiction before – the crashing of the waves of junkie narrative made me feel sick and disoriented. But *Monkey Grip* changed reading for me. For the first time I was consciously learning about *writing*. For the first time I was not reading for story (every so often I take up *Monkey Grip* to remind myself what happens in the 'end': Javo is a junkie; he continues to be a junkie; Nora continues to exist), but for words, for images, and for the way they were put together.

I reread it immediately. This time I read it more slowly, not feeling so ill, unmoored in the sea of the story. It was so unusual in its form, so intimate in its expression, that I needed to know how it was written.

Monkey Grip was met with some confusion and hostility by Australian reviewers, many of whom have lived to see their comments become part of the story of Garner's success (and the controversy she continues to stir up). The controversy centred not just on the fact that Garner was writing explicitly about sex and women's desire, but that she had based her 'novel' on her diaries. Had she simply copied out her diaries, rather than written a novel in the 'right' way? This was hotly debated at the time. There was no question that Garner had done something to the novel, had dismantled our idea of what it should be, what a plot was, what a beginning, middle and end should be.

Years later, Garner defended herself against this criticism in her famous article 'I', published in the journal *Meanjin*:

Shouldn't a real writer be writing about something other than herself and her immediate circle? I've been haunted by this question since 1977 when a reviewer of *Monkey Grip* asked irritably what the fuss was about: as far as he could see, all I'd done was publish my diaries. I went round for years after that in a lather of defensiveness: 'it's a novel, thank you very much'. But I'm too old to bother with that crap any more. I might as well come clean. I did publish my diary. That's exactly what I did. I left out what I thought were the boring bits, wrote bridging passages, and changed all the names. It was the best fun I ever had, down there in the domed Reading Room of the State Library of Victoria in 1976, working with a pencil and an exercise book on one of those squeaking silky oak swivel chairs. I'll never be that innocent again.

Certainly *Monkey Grip* reads like a diary, with its return and return to the same beginning, its characters repeating themselves in patterns of love, difficulty, disappointment, love, difficulty, disappointment. Is it a novel? The same question has been asked about her latest piece of fiction, *The Spare Room*. It is a question worth asking, and worth examining, but for the purposes of this essay, let me simply say that *Monkey Grip* was, for me, a new kind of novel; not just a random accretion of information, but a thoughtfully observed, deeply felt work of art about a woman who has been caught, as Garner puts it, in 'the gap between theory and practice'. The book is not just about loving a junkie; it is about trying to love and let go at the same time; trying to put into practice the idea of free love, of shared partners, and trying to be stoic about the kind of pain this causes. For me, at least, Garner had cracked narrative open. She had written, in a way, the kind of literature that Virginia Woolf had begun in her diaries and given full expression to in her fiction. She had followed a consciousness that did not bend easily into the more traditional shape of a novel. You could say she had written a women's novel.

In her *Meanjin* article Garner went on to say:

Why the sneer in 'All she's done is publish her diaries'? It's as if this were cheating. As if it were lazy. As if there were no work involved in keeping a diary in the first place: no thinking, no discipline, no creative energy, no focusing or directing of creative energy; no intelligent or artful ordering of material; no choosing of material, for God's sake; no shaping of narrative; no ear for the music of human speech; no portrayal of the physical world; no free movement back and forth in time; no leaping between inner and outer; no examination of motive; no imaginative use of language.

It's as if a diary wrote itself …

What Garner was doing with words was something I would attempt to do myself. She was working like a poet, with images. Plot is invariably secondary in Garner's work, and in her earliest fiction it is the image that is paramount.

This scene comes from the early pages of *Monkey Grip*:

We slept too lightly for rest. Early in the morning I climbed over him from the wall side of the bed, pulled my clothes on over my bloody legs, and wheeled my bike out his front door. A wild yellow sky, dry grey air full of turbulence. The street surfaces were burnished, blown clean as a bone. My bike tyres, pumped up hard, whirred on the glossy bitumen. Autumn, air, air, moving in dry warm blusters.

When I was younger these images altered the way I saw the world. They made me feel somehow *present*, alert to the shifts in light or weather, to the look of a street or a park or a house. A writer must be awake, and it was Garner who made me see this. She looked around her with an eye like a torch, sweeping across everything, pausing to select or reject, pausing to illuminate.

A great book is a companion, a friend, and like a friend it changes with you. When I was a teenager, *Monkey Grip* did not speak directly to my own experience – it taught me about life, gave me some idea of what was to come. But when I reread it, as I do most years, it makes me consider the life I am living now, with its similarities to Nora's (I have a daughter, lived for a long time in share houses, and am also a writer) and its great differences (I live with my partner and two children, and my experience with drugs and the miseries and pleasures of love affairs is a thing of the past). This passage, worth as much to me today as it was then, but changed now that I have changed myself, makes me consider how few of the day's deserted, illicit hours I currently inhabit. My life is more limited, more conventional than Nora's. If I am out at night or very early in the morning it is unusual. If I am I will look at the sky and note how thick the stars are (here in the mountains they prickle through the sky in their millions) or the quality of the new light. I will also notice how many people there are outside, pursuing their lives, when I am always, always indoors. This is reading, waking you up, reminding you of how you live: Garner's writing, speaking to me now more than thirty years after my first engagement with it, makes me remember my teens and twenties and treasure them, for all those empty hours, for the warm air full of turbulence and the street surfaces blown clean as a bone.

Since then, I have read every word that Helen Garner has published; the fiction so many times that her syntax seems entwined with my DNA. Somewhere in one of Garner's early books a girl holds a hose and 'whacks' the 'silvery rope' of water against a window. It is not possible for me to see a running hose without thinking of this moment. When I write sometimes Garner's sentences surface in my mind; I feel myself imitating a certain rhythm she has. I know I am not the only Australian writer who experiences this. Her language is embedded in my way of thinking, and in the way of thinking of many readers. We would be different people without her.

Did Garner influence me? The answer is yes, at first.

Bombora, my first novel, was written over a year or more, when I was in my early twenties. It is the story of a small family – father, mother and daughter. It is the mid-1990s. Leo is a musician, Madeline is a painter, and they live in a share house in inner-city Sydney – the suburb of Enmore, to be precise – in a large terrace that I'd once inhabited in London Street, which continues to provide me with material. I was living in Newtown by this time, writing whenever I could, retreating to my bedroom during the long slow days, sitting up at night when I'd come home drunk from a party, waking at first light to seat myself at the desk and begin again. I did not know what I was doing; I only knew that I was trying to get something right.

I'd started several novels and abandoned them, disgusted by the voice in them, the self-absorption, the lack of momentum. Then I began writing *Bombora*, at the scene with which it still begins, when the child character Annabelle is standing in a garden, feeling the absence of her mother. It is the day of her mother's funeral, but I did not know that when I started writing – all I knew was the phrase that found its way into the book: 'The absence was like a presence.' My own mother had not yet died, incidentally, and I am still intrigued by the power this phrase had to set me writing. Annie Dillard says:

One line of a poem, the poet said – only one line, but thank God for that one line – drops from the ceiling. Thornton Wilder cited this unnamed writer of sonnets: one line of a sonnet falls from the ceiling, and you tap in the others around it with a jeweler's hammer. Nobody whispers it in your ear. It is like something you memorized once and forgot. Now it comes back and rips away your breath. You find and finger a phrase at a time; you lay it down cautiously, as if with tongs, and wait suspended until the next one finds you . . .

While I was writing *Bombora* I was reading Helen Garner. I had all of her then-published fiction on the desk around me. I also had Dillard's *The Writing Life*, and I had my *Norton Anthology of Poetry*, which contained amongst its disparate riches the poems of Sylvia Plath. In his near-perfect story 'Love and Honour and Pity and Pride and Compassion and Sacrifice', Nam Le's eponymous writer-character says, 'For inspiration, I read absurdly formal Victorian poetry and drank scotch neat.' To me, the scotch and the poetry work in the same way: they induce intoxication, in just the right degree. The writer reads prose as though drinking clear water from a running stream, but poetry is meant to get you drunk.

I wrote *Bombora* as one should write all first novels – in a dream of pleasure. I can remember running up the flimsy stairs of the house I shared with my friend Patrick, smiling to myself. It was like coming back to a lover. The manuscript never rejected me – it was always glad to see me, always rich with possibilities, always ready for more complicated, thoughtful joy. I was twenty-four and I had been trying to write a novel since I was seventeen, but the ideas had kept drying up, stopping, running out, stalling. I am not sure exactly why the words suddenly began to work. It has to do, partly, with that first line occurring to me. And then the process that Dillard describes, laying down each following word or sentence and tapping it into place.

Perhaps I had reached a kind of critical mass with my own reading. I was so full of Garner that I needed, in a sense, to shed some of it. Or perhaps it was simply finding that elusive thing: a voice. Finding a voice is sometimes immediate, as in the moment that my line 'dropped from the ceiling', and sometimes can take years. You bait your line, you cast it: nothing bites. You re-bait, you cast, again and again. Sometimes you never get a bite, and eventually it is time to give up that project and turn to another.

Writing, when it is working, is about connecting – look, this joins to this, and this joins to this. I also remember the final edit I did on *Bombora*, before printing it out and sending it off. It came to me late at night that I needed to write, that I needed to reorder my narrative. I got out of bed in the dark and took the single step to my desk. I switched the light on, and then the little box of my Mac Classic. It seemed as though the novel hung in the air before me – I could see all of it, and almost without thought I moved scenes around, married one idea to another, joined my stories up. As Garner did (speaking back to her diary, to the way a life is actually lived), I had written discrete scenes that piled up, that formed narrative without recourse to the usual tools, without perpetually turning to the clock: *and then . . . the next day . . . when they got back . . . after the party.*

The effect is cumulative, rather than linear. Garner does not write, in *The Children's Bach* for instance, 'And then Athena and Dexter, Vicki and Elizabeth went to see Philip's band . . .' to open a scene that marks the first parting of ways for the married couple Athena and Dexter. Instead she writes:

Vicki spent an hour getting herself ready. She tied a diaphanous scarf round her head, stuck a yellow rose in it, and put a lot of makeup on her flat, smooth, pale face. She looked striking, and flustered because of the lipstick she had rubbed into her cheekbones.

Garner does not do bridges. We are left to find our own way into this scene – Vicki is going out – where is she going? Who is she going with? What will happen? It is the detail that carries us. We follow from one brightly coloured image to another, led like bees from flower to flower. I found this style enormously attractive. It was like poetry.

When I wrote *Bombora* I was influenced by Garner in a way that I am not influenced by anyone anymore – not Garner herself, not Alice Munro, nor George Saunders nor Kazuo Ishiguro, although I have read these writers every year of my adult life. I reread her deeply, greedily, as I was writing. I wanted to see how she did it, but I also wanted to feel the spell of her writing. It was a kind of enchantment.

Helen Garner is the author of four novels, two novellas, several collections of short stories and essays, three books of nonfiction, and most latterly, her published diaries. All of these remain in print. Martin Amis says, 'When we say we love a writer's work, we are always stretching the truth: what we really mean is that we love about half of it. Sometimes rather more than half, sometimes rather less.' I love more than half of Garner's work; more importantly, I respect every word of it. It is necessary, always, to read her closely, engaging with every sentence. Her writing, though never less than deeply political, is about *things*: the way they look, how the light falls on them. It does not lecture or harass, or try to curry favour. Garner looks around her and shows us what she sees. Her attention to the texture of life, to the silvery rope, to the 'juicy cough' of a granddaughter in *The Spare Room*, and to something as simple and as central as the weather, keep us intent, absorbed, on every page. In *The Children's Bach*, spring comes, and 'in the morning, when the first person opened the back door, the whole bulk of air in the house shifted and warmed'.

Sometimes I feel as though, without literature, I would have no memory. Reading this passage, I can see the open door in the Balmain house that Russell and I shared with our baby Alice. I look down the light-filled hall. Alice beetles along the carpet on hands and knees.

Still, it is not uncommon for me to find myself wishing that I did not have to record everything and could live my life in a kind of contented, animal silence. There have been times in my life when the detail, the multiplicity of things – and the urge to record them – has felt too much. I can't read Garner then – I can't read anything. I can't bear to keep noticing things. Like the tulips in Sylvia Plath's famous poem, the detail hurts me.

At other times, when the words are coming, when, as Garner once put it, 'the real stuff runs down our arm', it is as though there is nothing better in life, nothing more real nor more satisfying. This is when the conversation with other writers feels as alive as the conversations I have with living people. When they are companions as much as teachers. And Helen Garner can seem as much my parent as my own mother.

The difficulty is the point

I've just finished marking forty-odd exams, mostly written by people between the ages of eighteen and twenty-one. In them the students had to answer questions about aspects of literature such as writing in the first person, free indirect speech, genre, reading for landscape or gender or ethnicity. They also had to write an essay of one thousand words on the work of Helen Garner, Christos Tsiolkas, Judith Wright, Jack Davis or Tim Winton.

My students are, for the most part, education students who live in regional Australia. If they get their degree, they are bound for early childhood centres, preschools, primary schools, high schools. These will be our new teachers.

If you have little to do with tertiary education you might not have noticed that there is a whole new cohort of young people attending university, people who might not have done so thirty or forty years ago. Our economy has been transforming itself from blue to white collar for decades; an apprenticeship that relies on the written word is newly necessary.

Added to this, the university's relatively new status as a business – all universities are now forced to consider profit before anything else – means that it desperately needs students and will make it as easy as possible for everyone, anyone, to enrol. When I began teaching at this university the ATAR for education degrees was officially 60, but many students were entering the university through alternative pathways: TAFE, bridging courses at the university itself, written application. Universities are businesses. Students are customers. The more customers, the better the business does.

It follows that a business will want to retain its customers. The best way to retain a customer is to keep them happy. I'd suggest that happiness for students might arise from challenge, from hard work fairly rewarded, or from the acquisition of new and valuable skills. But there is of course a quicker route: you keep students happy by not failing them. And then – surprise! – when they graduate they are not literate, or numerate, or knowledgeable enough to perform the work they have been studying for.

But just because the horse has bolted doesn't mean we can't slam the stable door. And the way we do this in New South Wales is through the implementation of the compulsory

ACER Literacy and Numeracy test for Teacher Education, which students take at the end of their degree. They cannot graduate without passing it. For the past four years I have been teaching a subject designed to actively interrogate reading and writing abilities, and make students capable of passing the literacy part of their ACER test. Let's call the subject English One.

I find myself pausing here, to wonder why I am writing this essay. I have two burning concerns: one is to give readers an insight into what it is currently like to teach at an Australian university. To satisfy this concern I want to tell you about semesters and classes being shortened to save money on teaching; about passing incapable students simply to keep quotas up; about teaching students for whom attendance at university is no longer a necessary part of gaining a degree. This loops back to the idea of the university as business. Asking universities to stop making it easy for students to gain entrance and to pass is like asking Coca-Cola to slow down its sales. The logic of capitalism overrides everything in the new university.

The second concern is more abstract. I want to tell you about what it is like to teach literature to habituated non-readers, and why it is worth it.

Literature isn't, for me, a classroom. It is right at the centre of my life. I don't 'learn' from it. It isn't 'good for me'. It isn't work or study or a hobby. It *is* me. I think in lines from books I've read. It's alive in me all the time, I'm helpless, it runs through me like a torrent.

This is easy enough to communicate to other passionate readers. I was used to teaching literature to creative writing students, for most of whom reading, and reading widely, was a given. At the city university where I taught for more than fifteen years we read together like a pack of wolves, prowling a text for meaning, setting up a howl when we found a good sentence or a clever way of solving a structural problem. But with English One I had to slow my thinking down, separate it into parts. I did not at first know how much this would teach me. I did not realise that I would be learning too.

Possibly the single most important component of English One is compulsory attendance. Again, if you are not a student or an employee at a university you may not know this: that most universities no longer make attendance at tutorials and lectures compulsory. At other universities and in other subjects I have had to pass students who have attended no classes at all. Not distance or online students: internal students who live not far from the university. Some non-attendees do not learn enough to pass their subject; their non-attendance bites them on the arse, we fail them, everyone moves on. But many are able to access enough information about the course to pass. And no-one can say a word about the fact that they never came to university.

Spoonfed, I hear you say? Don't make me laugh. This is a feast of force-feeding, a Roman orgy of information and assistance, with students helpless and lolling while academics assist them in opening their mouths so the food can be tipped in, and then hold their jaws and help them masticate until it goes down. We keep asking ourselves why this generation is so anxious. There is more than one reason for this. But in part, this generation is anxious because *we* are anxious. We never let them do things alone: we intervene before they have had a chance to try, let alone succeed or fail. They lose confidence in their own abilities. They never get to feel the limits, or the limitlessness, of their real selves.

But in English One, students are only allowed to miss two classes out of the scheduled twelve without a documented explanation. Not only that, but if they don't pass the subject – they are allowed two attempts at this – they cannot take their ACER literacy test, and they cannot receive their degree. I can't tell you the difference this makes in a classroom. As a teacher, you feel traction: you feel as though you are doing something worthwhile. Your feet are firmly on the ground. These students need you, and they must learn what you have to teach.

The first assignment in English One is called a 'Reading Reflection'. It asks students to write about their reading habits: how often they read, what they read, what they feel they take from their reading. This assignment is only five hundred words long. It does two things: it starts the students' journey into *noticing* reading, thinking about their habits and what those habits mean for their academic future; and it tests their ability to write simple, straightforward sentences.

What have these students been reading before they come to our class? Some – a very few, and almost always women – have read nineteenth-century classics: the Brontë sisters, Jane Austen, George Eliot, Charles Dickens. Some – a very few, and almost always men – have read twentieth-century science fiction (Asimov and his ilk), and some of the Beats and their offspring: Kerouac, Burroughs, Bukowski.

The next and much larger group have read *The Hunger Games*, *The Curious Incident of the Dog in the Night-time*, *The Boy in the Striped Pyjamas*, some or all of the Harry Potter series, and a lot of autobiographies, either by sportsmen (the men) or by women who have been held in dungeons for years by rapists (the women).

The final group, about the same size as the group of *Hunger Games* readers, read their local newspaper, their Facebook pages and those of their friends, their newsfeed, and the occasional copy of a women's or a men's magazine. None, unless they have been made to by their high school English teacher, has read anything by an Australian author, unless it was Matthew Reilly.

More than once – in fact, every semester – I've had a student ask me in a sneering way why they have to read Australian literature for the course. The best method for dealing with this question comes from one of my academic friends. At the beginning of a class this friend asks his students to spend a little time imagining themselves as filmmakers or writers. He gives them a few minutes to think about the film or book they would make or write, and then asks them to describe it. He writes a one-line summary of each idea on the whiteboard. Then he points to the board and says, 'Look, Australian literature.'

If you don't anticipate this question, or deal with it constructively, you find yourself gasping with impotent rage as you try to explain why it is important that Australians have their own voices, why it might be good to resist American cultural imperialism; and a teacher gasping with impotent rage is not a good teacher. My best-received attempt at tackling this came when I heard myself saying to a class, 'It's as though you speak in Australian but dream in American.' I'm not entirely sure what I meant by this: I'm still considering it, wondering if it was just one of those Wildean epigrams that seem profound but finally mean nothing. Still, every person in the class lit up, nodding enthusiastically. It *sounded* true.

The first time I taught *Monkey Grip* in English One I was struck by two things. First, how many of my students were offended by it. They found it too sexually explicit, too full of 'profanity', and they deplored Nora's method of parenting: the shared household, the children exposed to drug taking and other radical behaviours.

The second thing that struck me was how *difficult* my students found the ten-page extract to read. They had no reference points, no context; they didn't know who Helen Garner was, the 1970s were too far away to mean anything to them, and they couldn't locate themselves in the story. They didn't know who was speaking, and who she was speaking to. How old was she, where was she, what was happening?

Here is the book's opening sentence:

In the old brown house on the corner, a mile from the middle of the city, we ate bacon for breakfast every morning of our lives.

If you are reading this essay, you're a reader. You probably know this sentence, and if you don't, you are comfortable with interpreting it. You can hear a character beginning to form: its romantic, optimistic, nostalgic voice; a voice yearning for simplicity; probably, in its deliberate imitation of a child's singsong, the voice of a woman, a mother. You know it might take a few pages to learn just who this woman is. You're skilled in this sort of patience.

But if you have never read anything more difficult than a Harry Potter book, how are you meant to proceed?

Well, there is only one way to go on, as I tell students – and that is to go on. This is the first and greatest difficulty they face. There's no reason for them to continue reading. There is so much else to read that is shorter, and not just aimed at them, but in the case of their Facebook feed, tuned to their experience. Marketed to them. Why would they bother reading something that was neither for them nor about them?

The British theorist and academic Mark Fisher writes:

> Ask students to read for more than a couple of sentences and many . . . will protest that they *can't do it.* The most frequent complaint teachers hear is that *it's boring.* It is not so much the content of the written material that is at issue here; it is the act of reading itself that is deemed to be 'boring'.

Pause for a minute. Return to that opening sentence of *Monkey Grip*. Be honest with yourself: it's easy. The words are almost all monosyllabic, the syntax is uncomplicated, the image is vivid. Now try this, the first sentence of Randolph Stow's 1965 novel *The Merry-Go-Round in the Sea*:

> The merry-go-round had a centre post of cast iron, reddened a little by the salt air, and of a certain ornateness: not striking enough to attract a casual eye, but still, to an eye concentrated upon it (to the eye, say, of a lover of the merry-go-round, a child) intriguing in its transitions.

You would have to say that this is not an especially enticing sentence. I find most students I teach are pulled up short by it. But who said everything has to be enticing? Mark Fisher says:

> Some students want Nietzsche in the same way that they want a hamburger; they fail to grasp – and the logic of the consumer system encourages this misapprehension – that the indigestibility, the difficulty *is* Nietzsche.

The difficulty is Stow. *The difficulty is the point.*

Here's how I teach this text, and every other one. First, we read it. Yes, students are supposed to come to class having read the texts, but many don't. Because of this, and because all of these students are planning, some day, to stand in front of a class themselves, I make them read aloud. One by one, the students stagger through the sentences. I correct them, try to nudge them along. I try not to pay attention to the blushing and giggling and the quavering voices. We go forward, through the difficulty.

Then, especially in the case of Stow, I go carefully through the text once more, line by line. First, I ask the students if they know the meanings of all the longer words. They generally don't. Using my classroom screen and an online dictionary, we look up 'ornateness' and 'transitions'. After this I talk about the context of the book, Stow as a writer, the arc of the story. Sometimes I draw a timeline on the whiteboard, showing them where we might plot Stow's work alongside other great works of literature or world events.

We return to the text. I remind them to look at the syntax. How many clauses are there in a typical Stow sentence? What effect does this have on our reading of it?

Then, once we've tried to use Stow's dense description to imagine the merry-go-round, I hand out whiteboard markers and I ask the students to come up to the board and try to draw what Stow has described.

It isn't really a method. I make it up as I go along. All I have to help me is the fact that my regional university hasn't yet caught up with the trend of cutting class times to save money on teaching. Our classes are two hours long, and I use nearly every minute. I'm not trying to *not* bore the students. I'm not trying to be what Fisher calls a 'facilitator-entertainer'. I'm trying to push past or through boredom, trying to show them the rewards of closely engaging with a text. In a way I'm just externalising the process I – and probably you – go through unconsciously every time I read.

Fisher says that many of his students are in a state of what he calls 'depressive hedonia'. He goes on to say:

Depression is usually characterised as a state of anhe-donia, but the condition I'm referring to is constituted not by an inability to get pleasure so much as it is by an inability to do anything else *except* pursue pleasure.

So I'm not trying to make them happy, or make them enjoy themselves. I'm trying to show them how critical engagement with literature enables critical engagement with living. I'm trying to interrupt what Fisher calls 'the constant flow of sugary gratification on demand'. And finally, I'm trying to help them pass that literacy test.

What have my students learned? Perhaps not much. Every semester several of them fail: some resist every line of questioning in tutorials, telling me over and over again that they see nothing in the texts I'm reading with them. I had a fourth-wall moment recently, which all teachers will be familiar with: that moment when the barrier between you and the class comes down, when you stand as yourself in front of them. I'd been trying to teach a student – let's call him James – whose response to questions like, 'What do you think the author was up to here?' had been a dogged and angry, 'No idea.' For the fifth or sixth time I approached him on one of my circuits of the class, and heard myself saying, 'What do you think, James? No fuckin' idea?'

We stared at each other. The class shrieked with laughter. We both blushed, and then we were laughing too, and I was apologising. But this moment broke something between us. James did not pass the subject; his written work was still not up to the job. He could not write – although he could speak, if he chose to – coherent sentences. But the work he handed in after this showed that he had tried, that he was sincerely attempting to understand the texts we were reading, and to notice their effects. I can tell the difference between a sincere assignment and an angry or cynical assignment; I've seen so many of both kinds.

But then there are moments like this, early on in my English One teaching, when my class were reading and struggling with Les Murray's 'The Cows on Killing Day'. I've always loved this poem. In it the poet imagines the death by knife of an old cow, from the point of view of the herd. Murray uses a first-person compound pronoun, 'all me', to speak in the cows' collective voice:

All me come running. It's like the Hot Part of the sky
that's hard to look at, this that now happens behind wood
in the raw yard. A shining leaf, like off the bitter gum tree
is with the human. It works in the neck of me
and the terrible floods out, swamped and frothy.

I had a young woman in my class who had already responded very positively to Helen Garner's 'Against Embarrassment', a simple essay that makes a plea for unself-conscious pleasure in performance. Like many students would after her, she had read Garner's essay in the light of her university enrolment; it made her determined to enjoy herself, to unself-consciously engage in learning, to stop being critical of herself. She'd worked several years as a dairy-maid after leaving school early, thinking she was 'too stupid' for university. As we read 'The Cows on Killing Day' aloud, her voice came ringing from a desk at the back of the class: 'But this is exactly what it's *like*!'

'The Cows on Killing Day' elicits a variety of reactions from my students, many of whom have been brought up on and are still living on farms. I've had young people furious with me. They say, 'I hate this poem. This shouldn't be written about,' or, 'No-one likes it. But it's a part of life.' I've also had city- or mountains-bred students – there are a couple of them each year – who've never killed an animal in their life, and self-righteously feel that the poem is a paean to vegetarianism.

But this student, the ex-dairymaid, read the poem as it is meant to be read. Murray doesn't ask for sympathy for the cow: his job is simply to use his art to show *what it's like*. After this class, my student went from a pass for her first assignment to a distinction for her second. At the end of the semester she told me she'd decided to switch her teaching specialisation to English.

This is what my students have learned: how to read more than two hundred words of a text at a time. How to write something about the way they feel. And finally – and maybe this is the only thing – how to notice that a text is *doing* something. Not to simply look passively at a block of writing, to slump, bored, in front of it and hope that it goes away. How to notice that it is up to something. Perhaps, in the future, to read a little differently. To feel those ideas about writing, so angrily learned, change the way they see.

They've also learned to relax a little about some of the things that upset them. What they call 'profanity'. Graphic descriptions of sex and masturbation. And interestingly enough, graphic descriptions of anger. *Loaded* in particular is a furious book. I love this line, spat out by Ari, Tsiolkas' young bisexual Greek man: 'I read the papers. I see the news. I talk to people; white, black, yellow, pink, they're all fucked.' When I was eighteen I felt the same way. Even now, it feels like a necessary part of growing up. In fact, it feels like a necessary part of *being* grown-up. You should always be ready to see what's fucked. But my students don't like it. Many of them choose *Loaded* to write about for their final essay because it is colloquial, fast-paced, easy to read; but almost all can't understand why Ari is so angry.

On a good day, I think they find Ari difficult because they themselves are generous people. They love their families, they are happy in the society they've been brought up in, and look forward to doing good when they work with children.

On a bad day, I think they find Ari difficult because the distinction between adults and teenagers has been blurred. We all want the same things now: phones, clothes, and food to photograph. We are all consumers. Teenagers don't want to stick it to the man anymore. They *are* the man.

Every couple of weeks I have lunch with two close friends, long-time academics, to compare experiences, to offload some of the stuff we've seen. It's the same all over. Every academic is caught between their principles and the rewards that come from abandoning them, between the demands of capitalism and their old role as guardians of higher learning. Teaching is valued less and less; our new god is management. And all corrupt systems must have their collaborators. The three of us have developed a language to describe these academics-turned-middle managers. We call them zombies. They stagger across the campus from meeting to meeting, a tickertape of acronyms flickering behind their undead eyes. Or we call them hosts, taken over by the parasite of neoliberalism. Of some we say they are more parasite than host. One of us described a particular administrator-academic as a 'glitchy half-person' – their self guttering like a candle, glitching between real person and corporate stooge.

When we come up with these ways to describe our experience we become more cheerful. One of these friends has recently been through a difficult confrontation with upper management. The three of us talked about the next administrative hurdle he had to leap and my friend said, 'I'm not getting involved. I'm powering down.' He made a sound like a building whose power has just been shut off, dropping his head and letting his arms go slack. The three of us began to laugh, as we always do when we're together, and soon we were wiping away rueful tears. For a moment there, we were in charge. Language is power, and when we find the right way to frame our experience, we're not being crushed by it.

This is what I want for my students. First, I want them to read a book all the way through. I want them to find something difficult and do it anyway. Then, I want them to notice what a powerful tool literature is, to understand that it helps us to know ourselves and the society we live in. I want them to discover that if they learn to handle language they might not feel as though they're worth nothing, have nothing to say. Finally, I want them to see that reading breeds thinking, and thinking breeds resistance, and surely, especially right now, that is a good thing.

Just anguish

A TV show I love is Jerry Seinfeld's *Comedians in Cars Getting Coffee*. It's a kind of comedians' *Paris Review* – a series of short interviews, conducted just as the title suggests, in cars and then in coffee shops. Seinfeld shows himself to be a gifted interviewer – recklessly personal, totally uninterested in self-promotion or in his interviewees' PR schtick, and, more than anything else, fascinated by craft, by words. I can't vouch for his sexual politics – I've seen too many interviews in which he and another male comedian compare ways of keeping the wife happy, and I nearly cringed myself out of the room when he asked queer comedic genius Kate McKinnon what she did when men were attracted to her. But this doesn't make me hate

73

him, or doubt him when I know he's saying something smart.

There's a moment in his first interview with the British comedian Ricky Gervais that I've watched a number of times. Like anyone else, I take pleasure in the sight of people laughing, of people uninhibitedly enjoying themselves – and these two certainly find each other funny. They're sitting in a cafe, and Gervais tells this joke about Hitler in his bunker:

> On the last day of the war, the Russians were advancing, they were two hundred yards down the road. He married Eva Braun, right, they had a cake and some champagne. They retired to bed early. In the morning he poisoned her, shot himself, and the gardener burnt the bodies. Now say what you will about Hitler, but that's a terrible honeymoon.

The two of them shake silently with laughter, unable to speak, and then Seinfeld, recovering himself, says, 'The funniest part of that joke is *Say what you will about Hitler*,' and they're off again, laughing uncontrollably.

What's significant to me about this exchange is not the joke, but Seinfeld reading the joke – understanding exactly what its pivot is, what's funny, how important the words are. *Say what you will about Hitler* – it's like a magician's suitcase, flipping open and open and open again. What do you mean, say what you will about Hitler? Is there more than one thing to say about Hitler?

These days, if you're getting any attention as a writer, you're getting most of it for your subject matter. I've sat on many, many writers' festival panels as an apparent expert on teenagehood or motherhood or teaching. I've had many kind people tell me I've changed their life by writing so openly about my vagina and my children. Of course I understand this. We all know the feeling of coming to a book and thinking, That's it! That's what I wanted to say – at last, someone has said it for me.

But I've recently realised that I don't go to Jane Austen or Helen Garner or James Wood to learn about life. I don't think, Elizabeth Bennet, you are my teacher, henceforth I will stand up to rude men. Although I am as religious as any other book lover about the books I love, it isn't *what* Austen writes about that really moves me, it's *how* she writes about it. In one of her superb early fragments, 'Love and Freind-ship', the brilliant fourteen-year-old Austen makes fun of the contemporary fashion for passionate friendship. This is a trope of Austen's: her books warn us to suspect any character who offers friendship before it has been able to properly and naturally take root. But look *how* she does it. Here is the first meeting of the two soon-to-be friends Laura and Sophia (from Laura's letter describing it):

We flew into each other's arms and after having exchanged vows of mutual Freindship for the rest of our Lives, instantly unfolded to each other the most inward secrets of our Hearts. – We were interrupted in the delightfull Employment by the entrance of Augustus (Edward's freind), who was just returned from a solitary ramble.

Never did I see such an affecting Scene as was the meeting of Edward and Augustus.

'My Life! my Soul!' (exclaimed the former) 'My Adorable Angel!' (replied the latter), as they flew into each other's arms. It was too pathetic for the feelings of Sophia and myself – We fainted alternately on a sopha.

I've had this image in my head my whole reading life. It's 'fainting' and 'alternately' that do the work here: they're timed so that the words flop forward one after another, just like the girls themselves: one, two, onto the sopha.

This is why I began writing: not just to unfold the inward secrets of my Heart, but to describe them accurately. To find the right words for them. When a writer finds the right words; when I can feel that they are interested in the pivot of a sentence, the seesaw of syntax, the right adjective; when they know to omit the adjective, and which verb will best illustrate movement on a reader's mental screen – well, that's when I'm happy. And there are few who do this better than the American writer S.J. Perelman.

*

Sidney Joseph Perelman, son of Sophie Charen and Joseph Perelman, both born in the 1880s in Russia, was born in Brooklyn, New York, in 1904. He was their only surviving child. His father's life did not embody the American dream – the businesses he opened, including a dry-goods store and a chicken farm, failed. Sophie and Joseph were socialists, they were readers, and they spoke both Yiddish and English at home. Sid did not speak fluent Yiddish but grew up amongst it, shall we say, just as all the American Jews of his generation did. He went to Classical High School in Providence and then Brown University, from which he failed to graduate because of being unable to pass trigonometry, despite three attempts. He began his publishing life as a cartoonist and moved on to short comic pieces. He wrote plays, screenplays and a novel. He was one of several screenwriters on two Marx Brothers films, *Monkey Business* and *Horse Feathers*, and won an Academy Award for his work on the 1956 film *Around the World in 80 Days*. He comes from a line of great writers: Robert Benchley, Dorothy Parker, E.B. White and James Thurber; he is a literary relative of Oscar Wilde, Noël Coward, Nancy Mitford, Max Beerbohm, Saki, and of course P.G. Wodehouse. His influence can be read directly in the work of Woody Allen, who was said to have once fallen on his knees in front of him in a New York restaurant; and the writer Donald Barthelme called him 'the first true American surrealist'. But he is remembered most fondly for his essays, what he called the *feuilletons*, or little leaves, which were published between the 1920s and the 1960s, predominantly in *The New Yorker*, but also in *Judge*, *Vanity Fair*, *College Humor* and *Life*.

At my grandparents' place in South Coogee – long since emptied of my family – my grandmother kept the bedrooms of my father and his sister in what I always imagined was a kind of still life of their occupation, which ended with their marriages in the early 1960s. My father's bedroom had dark green carpet. It smelt of books and of my grandparents and the sea, and it was where I always slept, annexing it as my own, when I stayed the night at the house. The room had a very simple wooden bookshelf, a single bed with a chenille bedspread, and a view due east from high up on the Coogee cliffs – the sea, the open sea, unfolding, unfolding, beyond eyesight. On the bookshelf were rows of old hardbacks and Penguins – and amongst these, or in fact making these up, were the humorists. S.J. Perelman and the Irish writer Patrick Campbell were the two I read most often, and S.J. Perelman is the one I've continued to read my whole life, throughout my apprenticeship as a writer, whenever I feel unhappy, whenever I need to relax. Some of these books stayed where they were, at my grandparents' house, but some lived with us. (I love to think of my parents' first proper date. They went to see the French film *La Belle Américaine*, and my mother laughed so much that she fell off her seat. And later worried that my father might think less of her for being so immoderate. Their marriage – not unlike my own, in fact – was forged in laughter. I suppose it is no wonder that humorists and comedians are the people I cleave to.)

There isn't anything I can say that will illustrate Perelman's brilliance so fluently as the work itself. And so, while planning this essay, I've been a bit like a monkey with a jar of peanuts – my hand is so full I can't get it out.

Perelman wrote several types of short comic essay. There were essays inspired by the absurdity of American advertising, which are, apart from anything else, an invaluable record of the explosion of stupidity that marks advertising's great boom years. You don't need *Mad Men* once you've read these. There are essays about his time as a scenario writer in Hollywood. There is a series, called *Acres and Pains*, which exaggerates and then documents the failures of his life with his wife and children on a farm in Erwinna, Pennsylvania. There's *Cloudland Revisited* – possibly my most treasured series – in which Perelman rereads the popular novels and rewatches the silent movies of his youth, which was smack in the middle of the Jazz Age. Here's a taste of his prose, from his essay about E.M. Hull's book *The Sheik* (a sort of Middle Eastern rape fantasy, which was also made into a movie starring Rudolph Valentino).

[W]hen, after a lapse of twenty-five years, I sat down recently to renew my acquaintance, I was heavy with nostalgia. A goodish amount of water had gone over the dam in the interim and I was not at all sure Miss Hull's febrile tale would pack its original wallop. I found that, contrariwise, the flavour had improved, like that of fine old port . . . Any connoisseur knows that a passage like 'She hated him with all the strength of her proud passionate nature' or 'I didn't love you when I took you, I only wanted you to satisfy the beast in me' acquires a matchless bouquet from lying around the cellar of a secondhand bookshop. No slapdash artificial ageing process can quite duplicate the tang. It must steep.

How beautifully the metaphor finds its apogee in that final, three-syllable sentence, which in turn balances out the complex syntax of the sentences that precede it. Perelman knows this: it must steep.

There are also the travel writings: *Westward Ha!*, about his travels around the world with the cartoonist Al Hirschfeld, and *Swiss Family Perelman*, a trip through Asia, Australia and New Guinea with his family, which I must say was not a happy one. Then there are the essays inspired by popular magazines of the era – magazines with names like *Spicy Detective*. There are the parodies of writers such as Raymond Chandler, who treasured his, and Dostoevsky. And then there are the weird surrealist pieces, inspired by single lines or ideas – 'Entered as Second Class Matter' or 'Scenario', in which Perelman stitches together clichés and lines from imaginary advertising campaigns and movies, creating peer-less montages of mid-twentieth-century American culture.

Here is an extract from the essay of Perelman's that I've reread the most times, and which has made me cry with laughter every time I do. It's from *Acres and Pains*, chapter thirteen, and it's about Perelman spending a night on his own at the farm.

Look friends, I'm just an ordinary country boy. I'm slow, and sort of quizzical, and as plain as an old board fence. I prize the quiet, homely things – applejack out of a charred keg, a bundle of faded securities, the rustle of old greenbacks. I love the scent of fresh-mown clover and the giggles that escape from it on a warm summer afternoon. But what I value most is solitude . . .

If rural life has done anything, it has taught me to be self-sufficient. I pity a man who can't be alone. There is nothing like a solitary evening in an old house, cooped up with one's dogs and books, to sharpen the senses and shorten the wind. One night recently, for instance, I suddenly felt I had to think things out and packed my family off to the seashore. It was ten above zero and building to a blizzard, but when I have to think things out I have no time for sentimental considerations. Breathing a sigh of relief, I double-locked the doors, barricaded them with bureaus and chairs, and set about preparing supper. I had some difficulty getting the beans out of the can, but I shortly contrived a serviceable bandage for my wrist and snuggled down in front of a crackling fire with the diaries of Wilfrid Scawen Blunt. I had read little more than three pages when I realised I was holding the diaries upside down and listening intently to a noise in the kitchen.

Loosely speaking, the sound combined a creak and a sigh suggestive of a musical saw. Now and again, it was smothered by a soft, mirthless laugh ending in a sharp click. My dogs, quick to guard their master, formed into a hollow square and withdrew under the couch. I dried my palms, which seemed to have accumulated a slight film of oil, and picked up the fire tongs. 'Who's there?' I inquired in a crisp falsetto. (After all, I thought, why waste a trip to the kitchen if nobody was there?) There was no answer; whoever it was didn't even have the common decency to reply. Angered, I strode toward the kitchen, whistling to warn of my approach, and flung open the door. Everything was in apple-pie order, including the apple pie, except that the rocking chair was bobbing slowly back and forth.

'That's odd – very odd,' I murmured, re-entering the living room and tripping over a chair. 'Probably caused by a draft from an open window or something.'

'Or something,' agreed one of the dogs from under the couch.

'Who said that?' I demanded sharply. The craven cur was frightened back into silence. I yawned casually, an effort that almost resulted in lockjaw, and consulted my watch. 'Well, guess I'll turn in,' I observed to nobody in particular. Hearing no objection, I started for the stairs, the dogs clustered about my ankles. A brisk, affable voice cut me short.

'The three homicidal maniacs who fled the county home for the insane are still at large tonight,' it said chattily. 'If you see a burly man of fifty with an ice pick –' I cannot abide petty gossip; switching off the radio, I went up the steps, taking them four at a time. It was a trifle close under the covers, especially as the dogs persisted in huddling in with me, but it made for a warm, *gemütlich* feeling.

It's hard for me to say just how much I've learned from Perelman, but even more importantly, it's hard to express just how much pleasure a piece of writing of this precision gives me. Perhaps the first thing to talk about is the way in which Perelman is absolutely prepared to leave you behind. You don't have to be a stranger to Perelman's era, his culture, or his home town of New York to need help keeping up with his cultural references and his astounding vocabulary. Perelman himself read everything; and he didn't just read everything, he remembered everything. Thus his work is salted with references to literature, dance, theatre, politics,

France, Russia, England, the Middle East, South-East Asia, not to mention the harvest of popular culture delivered every day by the newspapers and magazines he read.

When I first started reading his work at fifteen or so, the kind of challenge he flung at me was exactly what I was looking for. I gloried in how hard he was to understand, and because of this I felt a private relationship between him and me. I can safely guarantee it was exclusive; I didn't meet another person at Hunters Hill High who was reading him.

In this piece, Perelman hasn't paused to explain what *gemütlich* means, or who Wilfrid Scawen Blunt is, or even what the balconade is. (Perelman said of his use of Yiddish, 'There are nineteen words in Yiddish that convey gradations of disparagement, from a mild, fluttery helplessness to a state of downright, irreconcilable brutishness. All of them can be usefully employed to pinpoint the kind of individuals I write about.' This gives you a sense of the writer at work, interested not just in the almost right word, but the exactly right word – the one he picked from these 'gradations'.)

Nor, in this piece, does Perelman stop to say, 'I tried to open a can of beans and cut my wrist.' He bridges that small abyss between the opening of the can and the injury with 'I shortly contrived a serviceable bandage for my wrist', and dares us to cross it and follow him. Nor does he bother to explain why freshly mown clover might have giggles escaping from it.

Perelman himself said:

People who like my work have to understand words and their juxtaposition as well as the images they create. It's very hard to make a person laugh who doesn't have inside him the words I use. My humor is of the free association kind, and in order to enjoy it, you have to have a good background in reading. It's a heavy strain for people who haven't read much.

But he was forgetting, when saying this, that his writing could teach reading, as it did for me. I had a good vocabulary for a fifteen-year-old – but a much better one once I'd read Perelman.

So, if I am so heavily influenced by Perelman, and such a lover of comedy, why not write comic *feuilletons* myself? Well, the truth is that a writer does not choose their form – it chooses them. I'm not suggesting total helplessness; Perelman himself is testament to the fact that comedy comes in many shapes – the script, the essay, and even the novel were forms he mastered. But when asked why he didn't use his astounding talents to write more novels, he said:

It may surprise you to hear me say – and I'll thank you not to confuse me with masters of the paradox like Oscar Wilde and G. K. Chesterton – that I regard my comic writing as serious. For the past thirty-four years, I have been approached almost hourly by damp people with foreheads like Rocky Ford melons who urge me to knock off my frivolous career and get started on that novel I'm burning to write. I have no earthly intention of doing any such thing. I don't believe in the importance of scale; to me the muralist is no more valid than the miniature painter. In this very large country, where size is all and where Thomas Wolfe outranks Robert Benchley, I am content to stitch away at my embroidery hoop. I think the form I work can have its own distinction, and I would like to surpass what I have done in it.

Perelman's writing is not the kind you use to write a novel, which needs expansion, exposition, room to accommodate more than a single idea precisely followed. An entire novel maintaining the precision of a Perelman sentence – well, it's hard, if not exhausting, to imagine. It only occurred to me as I was writing this piece that my relatively recent addiction to the short story comes directly from this addiction to Perelman's work. I have a lot to say about the way people behave next to each other, but nothing that needs a hundred thousand words to say it in. I've sat down to the embroidery hoop and I'm not sure I'll ever get up.

Still, let's not pretend it's always fun. I often find myself recalling a brilliant interview with the novelist Jessica Anderson, a contributor to Kate Grenville and Sue Woolfe's invaluable writing handbook *Making Stories*. Anderson, asked about what she does when she's finished a book, describes feeling only relief. 'I hate writing, don't you?' she says. 'I hate it.' I think this might apply to almost all the writers I know – it certainly applies to me, and to Perelman. From an early age I've been compelled to record things; I've still got my diaries from the time I began reading him, and I find that in them I'm writing out sentences over and over again, changing words to see which sounds best, which way the sentence tilts. But when it comes to the business of starting work on something, well, there's pretty much anything else I'd rather do. And Perelman was no different. If he was paid well for an assignment – a script, a series of essays, a TV or radio show – he would take a break afterwards, writing nothing for months. Asked if there were any devices that he used to get himself going, he answered, 'Just anguish.' He went on to say:

> Just sitting and staring at the typewriter and avoiding the issue as long as possible. Raymond Chandler and I discussed this once, and he admitted to the most bitter reluctance to commit anything to paper. He evolved the following scheme: he had a tape recorder into which he spoke the utmost nonsense – a stream of consciousness which was then transcribed by a secretary and which he then used as a basis for his first rough draft. Very laborious. He strongly advised me to do the same . . . in fact became so excited that he kept plying me with information for months about the machine that helped him.

This gives me the opportunity to showcase Perelman's parody of Chandler, reportedly adored by the crime author. This is from 'Farewell, My Lovely Appetizer', first published in the mid-1940s.

I came down the sixth-floor corridor of the Arbogast Building, past the World Wide Noodle Corporation, Zwinger & Rumsey, Accountants, and the Ace Secretarial Service, Mimeographing our Specialty. The legend on the ground-glass panel next door said, 'Atlas Detective Agency, Noonan and Driscoll,' but Snapper Driscoll had retired two years before with a .38 slug between the shoulders, donated by a snowbird in Tacoma, and I owned what goodwill the firm had. I let myself into the crummy anteroom we kept to impress clients, growled good morning at Birdie Claflin.

'Well, you certainly look like something the cat dragged in,' she said. She had a quick tongue. She also had eyes like dusty lapis lazuli, taffy hair, and a figure that did things to me. I kicked open the bottom drawer of her desk, let two inches of rye trickle down my craw, kissed Birdie square on her lush, red mouth, and set fire to a cigarette.

'I could go for you, sugar,' I said slowly. Her face was veiled, watchful. I stared at her ears, liking the way they were joined to her head. There was something complete about them; you knew they were there for keeps. When you're a private eye, you want things to stay put.

Well, this makes me very happy.

Once, in my late teens, I was introduced to Ike, the father of my friend Josh. I had been taught to be terrified of him by our other friends because he was important and busy, and in no way approachable. He was just Ike, and he wasn't interested in us. Josh lived in an enormous house in Vaucluse, a house with wings and staircases and lookouts and a swimming pool. I'd been to the house several times without encountering Ike – he was always buried some-where in the distant reaches of the building, or pulling up in his Porsche just as we were heading downstairs to Josh's bedroom. But on this day he walked in before we could walk out and Josh, suddenly formal, said, 'Dad, this is my friend, Tegan Bennett.'

Ike sniffed, eyes glinting behind his glasses, and said, 'Tegan Bennett. That's a good Jewish name.'

It was one of those moments when your brain actually assists you instead of snatching the rug out from under you. Without a beat I answered, 'I do my best.'

Ike *smiled.* Then Josh seized me by the hand and dragged me downstairs, where he said, '*That's* how to speak to my dad.'

It was one of the proudest moments of my life, and I have total recall of it. It was the words: getting them right.

Detail II

Every week, if we can manage it, I go for a long walk with my friend Vikki. We first met when our sons, now fourteen, were toddlers. We used to be pushing prams, but now it's just us. The shape of Vikki's life is quite different from mine: she's had a third child, and she is that old-fashioned thing, a homemaker. She makes her own bread and yoghurt, she knits and sews, she doesn't have a smartphone. This sounds intolerable, but she is one of the least smug, most capable, most alive and interesting people I have ever met. Her favourite book is *Moby-Dick*. She once resuscitated her son after he fell, during a seizure, into a pool.

What is the point of these meetings? It's not just the reaffirming of our affection for each other – it's the exchange of detail. What Vikki has to tell me and what I have to tell her is the small stuff about how we keep our boys on track at home and school, how we keep our girls upright through this medieval HSC year, what we do when we lose our temper with our children. We tell each other things as a kind of absolution. It's an open and equal swap – here is my shit, in exchange for yours.

Two months before my mother died of lung disease, Vikki came over to my house. She sat down on the couch and said in an uncharacteristically flat, almost sarcastic voice, 'Well, snap. My mother's got lung cancer.'

This seemed unfair, and too coincidental. But life doesn't care about coincidence or unfairness. Vikki's mother died four months after mine.

I suppose my mother's official dying began a week before the actual death. It was nearly three years since she had been diagnosed, and a year at least since she'd been attached permanently to an oxygen machine. When she left the house – which she didn't, at all, in the last three months of her life, as it was too terrifying for her – she had to be pushed in a wheelchair with a little oxygen bottle between her knees, or we could pull one behind her on a trolley. But at home she was attached to a machine the size of a bar fridge, which sat in the long gallery that joined one end of the house to the other. It was an oxygen concentrator, a device that didn't need to be refilled or replaced like the bottles; it compressed the air in the house into pure oxygen, which was what Mum needed to survive. Its motor had a timbre like an air-conditioner or an old gas heater – as though the house itself was breathing, humming. After Mum's stay in hospital some months earlier, we'd brought home a humidifier, which warmed and dampened the oxygen running into the prongs in her nose. Previously the air had been cold and dry. This makes the nasal passages dry out and become permanently sore. These side effects become torture over time.

All this meant that for more than a year Dad had slept beside someone whose repose, when it was repose, was permanently noisy. When it was not repose it was often panic – if Mum moved too quickly, her slowly closing lungs missed their chance to draw in air and she would find herself as though suddenly thrust underwater, and as frightened, every time, as though this had actually happened. Together Mum and Dad had lain awake in the nights with the lamp on my mother's side of the bed switched on, making a little bell of golden light in their room. I'd seen them, from the dark lounge room at the other end of the gallery. Together they spent those wakeful hours talking about – well, I don't know. This is a volume of exchanges owned only, now, by Dad.

When he called to ask my sister, my brother and me to come down together, we knew it would not be long. A week, perhaps two weeks. Please god no more. It is a condition of caring for the dying that you simultaneously cannot bear

to have them die and cannot bear for them to live one day longer. I'd made the mistake, late in the piece, of going into an online forum on pulmonary fibrosis, Mum's odd, incurable disease. It was an American forum, as the disease had not yet gained much attention in Australia. I was horrified to learn how long it took some people to die. One woman posted that her father had had 'three last Christmases'. We'd just had a 'last Christmas' ourselves and it felt as though we had used up the store of optimism that brings any family together for special occasions. Funny how the spontaneous coming together of two or three of us was always easier. Funny how each family keeps plugging away at the organised fun. I simply could not imagine us doing it again.

I had wished for a long time that she would die. Not just because I loved her and didn't wish her to suffer – which

I did, and which I didn't – but because *I* didn't want to suffer.

Two things I remember about that day – my brother saying he would go first. I was so grateful to him. I seem to remember watching him pack, but I can't have, as he was in his house and I was in mine. I have a vision of him thrusting things into a duffel bag and heading for the car.

I also remember standing in the back room of our house, a dark little room, the square of window glowing bluely at the edge of my vision, and saying to my husband that it was time, and that I had to go. He took my hands or my arms and said, 'Do you want to wait? Do you want to see what Joss says when he gets down there?' and I answered, 'I can't have this conversation.' I knew that I'd reached a point where I could no longer make a decision for myself. Until then I'd thought carefully about every move, planned it around our weeks of teaching and writing and looking after the kids. Russell nodded, kissed me, and my own bag was packed.

We three siblings made an agreement, easily, which was not like us – our way of deciding something can often be an awkward dance of each of us giving way until no-one gets what they want. We decided that at least two of us would be in Sydney with Dad and Mum, while the other spent a night at home. We would take it in turns. All three of us live within ten minutes of each other in the Blue Mountains town of Katoomba. (This was not a decision either.

Our six children have grown up near each other, and this has been good, but we didn't do it on purpose. It fell out that way.)

Mum and Dad's house is in a laneway, built on a narrow block. It is a long house, full of sliding panels and rooms as open as they can be to the Sydney air. You need to leave Sydney for a colder climate to discover just how subtropical a city it is. Climbing out of my car, I always notice the heavy scent of lantana, feel the weight of the air.

In those first few days people came and went, bringing food. Two or three of us would sit at the table in the kitchen, talking and sighing. Eventually one of us would heave themselves to their feet and head back up the gallery to Mum's room, to relieve whoever had been sitting there with their knitting or their book. We didn't like to leave Mum alone too much. We sometimes wished we could.

After a couple of days it was time to move Mum from the bed she shared with Dad into the bedroom next door, where we'd installed a hospital bed so that we and her nurses could reach her easily, could help in the very last stages of her life. First we had to arrange the paintings in the second bedroom, taking some down, hanging others. We brought painting after painting for her to choose from. She chose, amongst others, a painting she had done of a doorway through which you could see another doorway, looking into an obscured distance as though into a mirror.

I'm not sure if she chose this one because it was comforting, because she saw something in the idea of looking out, through the doorways, to somewhere not yet reached, or whether she chose it because she hadn't quite finished it and was still 'reading' it, looking for its solution. My nephew took photos of the walls in the second bedroom with Mum's iPad, then brought it back to her so she could approve the set-up.

She was conscious then, of course, and talking to us, and sitting up against her pillows, but dazed, as though she'd just been woken up. Sometimes she would drift away, eyes closed, even while she held a teacup or your hand.

My brother took charge of the moving, which Mum had been terribly frightened of. Even shifting in bed made her gasp and choke. I can't remember how she was moved – she must have been carried by two of us, arms crossed under her – but my brother invented a narrative to help her cross from one room to the other. It was exactly the kind of thing she would have done herself. He told her she was in the surf, and with each wave – each wave of not being able to breathe, which was now a natural result of any kind of movement – she was to think of herself ducking under that wave. It takes confidence, early earned by many fortunate children of this country, to crash headfirst into a wall of water. This confidence would be useful to Mum. As she was carried, my brother chanted, 'And – *under*! And – *under*!'

*

People continued to visit. I went home for one night and felt perfectly safe, fenced about by my husband and two children, and then I went back. Two more nights passed in the long house and it was my time to go home again.

But things were looking different. I was sitting by the bed with Mum's doctor, who had visited her every single evening for nearly six months. I had heard of gifted doctors, and I had met nurses – including Prue, who had been with us at home for the last few months – who could hold and move a patient as though they were a baby and the nurse a perfect parent: strong, unyielding, gentle. But this doctor did something I'd never seen before. When he came to see Mum he would sit down on the edge of her bed. He would take her hand, and then her whole arm, in his. He would run his fingers up and down her arm and look at her, talking to her. He was reading her as Mum might read a painting. His eyes travelled up her arm, looking at her veins. He put the back of a hand to her cheek. He listened to what she was saying, but also to the sound of her voice. I've never seen anyone so alive to another human being.

I said to him, 'I can't decide whether to go home.' By this stage Mum had had her last moments of consciousness; now she was asleep, taking long, racking breaths.

This was an interesting moment. I don't know what other doctors would have done, but this one had shown himself to be the kind of person who would not make your choices for you. He refused to offer certainty when there was none, even when his very presence induced such dependence on his opinion. I knew this – I'd begged him a few times over the previous months to tell me when Mum was going to die. He couldn't – and so he wouldn't. But we were somewhere different now.

He was holding Mum's hand, stroking her arm, and he said, 'What do you need to go home for?'

I shrugged, as a way of trying to halt a sudden onslaught of tears. 'See my kids,' I managed.

He nodded. He looked at me. I looked at him.

'I think I'll stay,' I said.

He nodded again. 'Might be a good idea.'

It was terrible, feeling it get dark. All the friends and relatives – my cousin Lisa, my cousin Mandi – had retreated, leaving us with food. One of us put on a favourite film in the living room – *Withnail and I*. We decided we would drift back and forth to the film, taking breaks when we needed to. Over the next months our way of raising a fist at the world would be to shout at one another, 'The fuckers will rue the day!'

Mum was dying in the room her sister Catherine had died in fifteen or more years earlier. We'd taken turns sitting with Cath just as we were with Mum now, although back then it was Mum who did most of the sitting. When, some months earlier, we'd had to decide where Mum would die, I was the one who volunteered to have the conversation with her. My father would have been able to find a place for Mum in a comfortable hospice; he could also afford to have her cared for at home. The choice was hers.

I sat on Mum's bed and asked her to think about the fors and againsts of being here, in her own house. I knew already that that was what she wanted – I knew where we were headed. I think it is what I would have chosen myself, although it would not have been easy. Mum had liked being in hospital, where it seemed everything could be done, and done by people who did not drop bedpans, trip over oxygen tubing, or rush off to cry in the bathroom.

'Here's an against,' Mum said. 'I don't want this to be the house of dead ladies.'

I thought for a moment. On most subjects, Mum was utterly fearless. You could try her with any thought and she would listen. Curiosity almost always conquered any natural anxiety or reticence she might have felt. So it was important to give her the same attention, to consider carefully just what she was saying. 'Do you mean,' I said after a minute, 'in a real estate sense? Or in a sort of spiritual sense? Like a haunting?'

She gave me a withering look. 'Real estate. The house might be difficult to sell if two people have died in it.'

I knew what she meant. I knew the people in the lane were aware she was dying; their kindness, and their quiet voices as they walked past the house, were testament to that. But I also knew that none of them had been here fifteen years ago, when Cath had died, and that perhaps none of them would be when Dad wanted to sell the house.

Neighbourhoods were not what they had been. Houses that we still referred to as the Wilsons' or the Browns' had had three, four, five families come and go since we'd lived at home. I knew nobody would be thinking of Mum's house as the house of dead ladies.

It was dark. I can't seem to stress this enough. And around two or three in the morning I began to feel sick. Not just a bit dizzy, but wavering, wobbling, and with a thick feeling in my throat as though I was going to throw up. Oh god, I thought, I've got some sort of gastro. I'm going to be sick, I'm going to be sick. I had to get up and leave the bedside. I went into Mum and Dad's room and lay down in the dark, my eyes so accustomed to it that the furniture stood out like bones in a crypt. I was flat on my back. My sister came to lie beside me and I said, 'You can't lie here. I have to be alone.'

If I could go back and change one thing about the way I managed my mother's dying, it would be my *tone*. Not just the tone I used to my brother and sister and father, but the tone of my whole self. Early on I had decided that I would be the best at this. I was convinced I was the best. I would be the most capable. I would be the one who did not give way to tears when our mother was in distress. I kept to this tone throughout, and that night was the first night I began to notice that it was more than a tone. It was a thing, a clenching thing, an instrument. An instrument I used against myself. I was my own iron maiden, closing, driving the spikes of myself into myself. My friend Gabrielle Carey, whose mother had died some years before, looked searchingly at me one day and said, 'Make sure you take some time to rest. Do something for yourself.' That's what I *am* doing, I thought, closing harder.

I lay next to my sister with the iron maiden closed over me, and my brother came into the room. 'Are you okay?' he said.

'I'm sick,' I said and made myself reach a few inches across the mattress to hold my sister's hand. 'I think I've got gastro or something.'

From the real sick room, the breaths, long, racking breaths. From the gallery, the long hum of the oxygen compressor.

'You're not sick. You're tired. You've overdone it,' said my brother.

He made me stand up, and led me down the gallery to the kitchen, where the lights were switched on. He took a little container of Valium out of his pocket and unscrewed its lid.

'I don't need that,' I said. 'I can't afford to be sleepy.'

'Have half,' he said, and expertly snapped one in two. He handed it to me, ran me a glass of water. I put the pill in my mouth, drank the water. I stood looking at him, and he at me. Quite suddenly, I didn't feel sick anymore.

'Back we go,' he said.

*

Mum was little, and now littler than ever, her body like a stick under the covers. She was yellow, her eyes sunk deep into her face, the sockets dark as though someone had used charcoal to colour them in. Her mouth was permanently half open, the lips stretched dryly across it. We kept applying pawpaw cream, but her lips had no softness or malleability. They were like the rubber seal of an old pickling jar. Her head was jerked sideways, at an angle that looked painful. Once in the previous days, I'd slid a hand under her neck and tried to straighten it to an angle that looked less uncomfortable, and she'd made a noise somewhere between a squawk and a shriek. I left it alone after that.

We sat in a half-circle around her bed, listening to her breath crackling and gargling and growling. She did not seem closer to death, or further away from it.

At three or four am, ten or at the most fifteen minutes after we called him, the doctor arrived, looking weary. He stood next to Mum. He held her arm, ran his thumb along it, looked her up and down. Then he reached over Mum's face, slipped a sure hand behind her head, unhooked the tubing from around her ears, and took the oxygen prongs out of her nose.

We stared.

'She doesn't need it anymore,' he said.

We had not seen Mum's face without oxygen gear attached to it for more than a year. It looked – clean.

The doctor stepped out into the gallery and switched the oxygen machine off.

Silence. The silence of a landscape over which a goods train has passed, dragging a line of carriages that it seemed would never end. Silence that carried the imprint of a sound so long heard it was as though you were still hearing it. Silence, except for the sound of Mum taking her dying breaths.

Nothing changed. We sat a long time, saying nothing, upright in our chairs but half sleeping, while the night solidified around us.

The first hint of light. I had been holding Mum's hand with my eyes closed, and I thought I was asleep, but a sudden pulse shot through me, and I was speaking before I was looking, saying, 'She's dead.'

As I was standing up, leaning over her, I saw something leap up, a little light like a flame, from Mum's face, perhaps from her mouth. Later I would think of the *ignis fatuus*, the little spurt of phosphorus from a marsh, gas that spontaneously combusts in air, once mistaken by travellers for a ghost. Then, although I have no religious belief, I thought of it as the last sign of Mum, escaping, disappearing. And suddenly everyone was crying except the doctor, who stood by her, looking into her dead face, the lips finally slack, the head dropped back, glancing at his watch, and smoothing the hair back from her head.

In a short time we composed ourselves, and it was getting light, and the doctor was writing the death certificate. As he left, he said to us, 'I've seen a lot of deaths, and this is in the top five per cent.' We were all grateful; we knew he was right, even though it had been so terrible. And later, we amused ourselves or lightened things when talking of Mum and her dying by giving each other the thumbs-up. 'Top five per cent!'

There is more to tell: the dressing of Mum, the arrival of the gentle people from the mortuary with their fold-up trolley and the body bag, and me hiding in the bathroom so I didn't have to see her being packed up. I drove home later that day. It was a great comfort to see my children and my husband. I didn't yet know how hard it would be to force my iron maiden open, how much trouble lay in front of me. I went to bed early, exhausted.

Another important part of the exchange between Vikki and me is labour stories. She has three, I have two, and we have each had a miscarriage. We tell them over like beads, each hour carefully recalled.

I remember my friend Kate, whose first child was born six months before mine, looking me in the eye after her labour and saying, 'Tigs, it's *terrible*' – a truth that was to be of great help to me.

After Mum died, I wanted to say the same thing to Vikki: 'Vix, it's *terrible*.' But this was the only time I couldn't tell her the details. Her mother, Brenda, having had the most painful and degrading treatment for her cancer, was becoming worse, not better. What to say to Vikki about those last weeks and days? I could only give advice. Get some sleep. Make sure to eat. One detail we did share in Brenda's final week, both finding relief in laughter: each family had had an attack of nits on the deathbed. Both of us had alternated hand-holding and brow-wiping with nit-combing.

The day after Mum died, I was woken at five am by the sensation of rising on water, as though I had been lying in the bed of an empty dam and it had suddenly filled. What was filling, I realised as I awoke, were my eyes, with tears; they brimmed over even before I knew where I was.

My husband woke too and turned his body to face mine. He laid his arm alongside me and pulled me over until I was lying across it, against his body. And in this way I told him every detail of that last night, pausing only to wipe away the tide of tears that kept rising and rising. It took an hour or more, while the children were still sleeping. I told him all that had happened, and he listened carefully. It was the single kindest thing anyone has ever done for me.

The worst that could happen

Three days shy of her fifteenth birthday, Alison Pope paused at the top of the stairs.

Say the staircase was marble. Say she descended and all heads turned. Where was {special one}? Approaching now, bowing slightly, he exclaimed, How can so much grace be contained in one *small package*? Oops. Had he said small package? And just stood there? Broad prince-like face totally bland of expression? Poor thing! Sorry, no way, down he went, he was definitely not {special one}.

These are the first lines of the first story in George Saunders' *Tenth of December*. In this story, 'Victory Lap', Alison Pope continues her descent of the stairs, talking to herself, and opens the back door to a man in a meter reader's vest, a man who is a rapist and murderer, and who is there to rape and murder her.

George Saunders, the bestselling author of four collections of short stories, a novella, a novel, a children's book and a collection of essays, began his professional life as a geophysicist, working for the Radian Corporation while he completed an MFA in creative writing at Syracuse University. His teachers included Raymond Carver and Tobias Wolff. Saunders now teaches at Syracuse.

In the documentary *Bad Writing* (2011), made by an ex-creative-writing student in search of insight into his own execrable poetry and fiction, Saunders accuses himself of having a 'big Hemingway boner' when he began his degree. In another interview, he says he spent a year writing a 'serious novel' with all the skills he had learned at college, and those he had picked up from Hemingway, Jack Kerouac and Thomas Wolfe. When he had finished, he reread it and hated it. It was 'horrible, incoherent'. One day at work, during a conference call, he began 'neurotically scribbling out these Dr. Seuss-like poems, and when I got to the end, there was more energy in that than anything I'd written in the last three years. That was my breakthrough.' He describes it as not so much a shift in genre as in 'tonality'.

I first read Saunders' work in 2000, when a teaching colleague gave me a copy of his second book of short stories,

Pastoralia. I had just begun an uncertain apprenticeship in the short story – through teaching it. There is no question that *Pastoralia* turned this apprenticeship into a full-time job, a life's work. It felt as though every short story I had read previously was a kind of nothing, a dribbling away of narrative, a useless entrainment of pretty words. Truman Capote tells us to ask of the short story: 'After reading it, can you imagine it differently, or does it silence your imagination and seem to you absolute and final? As an orange is final. As an orange is something nature has made just right.' Saunders' stories appeared to me as though I had never seen an orange, or only a poorly imagined one, a pale one, a painted one. Suddenly I knew what an orange *was*.

The classic Saunders story, like a classic Dr. Seuss, is most easily distinguished by the author's use of language, where he is brilliantly at work on several levels. Saunders has what Thomas Pynchon described as 'an astoundingly tuned voice'. His characters, for the most part struggling, under-educated people dreaming of better things, speak to themselves as clearly as they can, but their language is either mangled or colonised by another language: of the corporation, of advertising, of the self-help manual. More often than not they use polysyllabic words, incorrectly. No-one understands so well as Saunders that clarity of speech means clarity of thought, and that these things together mean power.

Saunders' characters are powerless but always hoping, incoherently, that this might change.

Alison Pope is a middle-class girl in a comfortable house, but like all teenagers she is trying, through a kind of self-narration, to arrange reality into something less banal, less awkward. Something kinder. Alone in the house, she is telling herself a story that will carry her right down the stairs. But because she is not completely in charge of her own language she has to keep pulling up, correcting herself. That wasn't {special one} the first time, with the business about the small package – the story got out of control. So she begins again:

> What about this guy, behind Mr. Small Package, standing near the home entertainment center? With a thick neck of farmer integrity yet tender ample lips, who, placing one hand on the small of her back, whispered Dreadfully sorry you had to endure that bit about the small package just now. Let us go stand on the moon. Or, uh, in the moon. In the moonlight.

This clearly isn't {special one} either, and Alison has to keep returning and correcting, returning and correcting until she reaches the door, where a truly unkind reality awaits – one that she is absolutely unable to organise into something better. And here we switch to the point of view of Kyle, her teenage neighbour, whose mental space is colonised by the voices of his panic-stricken, control-freak parents. Kyle sees Alison in trouble, but he knows that to help will be to violate his parents' countless 'directives', which preclude running in the yard, leaving the yard barefoot, and entering the Secondary Area – beyond the yard – without permission.

The state of Kyle's household, with its directives and Traffic Logs and Work Points, is an example of Saunders' magical ability to dream up little societies or near-future situations and furnish them with products and sets of rules that instantly cohere into a logical world. Nothing takes place in space, or during the Middle Ages, or on an earth transformed by climate change, but he is a world-builder par excellence, one of the most truly speculative writers of fiction at work today. When Saunders writes the future, he creates situations that feel a terrifying hair's-breadth from our own. He seems not to be predicting so much as anticipating: a subtle difference.

Saunders' biggest, widest target is capitalism, and at his best he makes you notice, as though you had only just noticed, how money and the art of selling things (and the helpless way we go on buying things) have come to govern everything we do. All of his characters are victims of capitalism in some way – from the teenage boy in 'Jon', from *In Persuasion Nation* (2006), who has a device fitted to the back of his neck that runs advertisements continuously through his brain and is given a constant supply of mood-altering drugs to help him 'evaluate' them, to the character in 'Sea Oak', from *Pastoralia* (2000), who is fired from his job as a waiter and stripper but shouts desperately, 'It's been a pleasure!' as he leaves, because there is so little work available and he is 'trying not to burn any bridges'. Endless satisfaction and instruction are to be received from Saunders' lists of invented product and place names, television shows and theme parks. I like KnyghtLyfe™, a drug that enables its user to speak in the language of chivalry (necessary if you have a Medicated Role at a medieval theme park), and the television shows *How My Child Died Violently* and *The Worst That Could Happen*. This is the anticipatory impulse in Saunders' writing – it is scarily easy for us to imagine drugs or television shows like these. He is always reminding us of what could be: in effect, the worst that could happen.

Saunders' first published book, *CivilWarLand in Bad Decline* (1996), received a lot of attention for the aforementioned elements – its interest in capitalism, alternative worlds and, most of all, theme parks – but also for its darkness. The words 'dark' and 'bleak' are used again and again in reviews of this collection, and indeed Saunders is unsparing when it comes to laying out grim futures, or non-futures, for his characters. It is very much a first book, in which we can see the author testing his skills, trying out his tricks. On the first page we hear about 'Burn 'n' Learn', a company that arranges for you to tan in a fully stocked library where high school girls on rollerskates fetch books for you. Ideas proliferate in this collection, but the body count feels unnecessarily high and the endings are grisly and a little unwieldy, the author putting a gun to his characters' heads out of what feels a bit like uncertainty.

Pastoralia contains some of Saunders' best stories – most significantly 'Sea Oak' and the title story, in which a man has a job as a live-in caveman in an ancient-history theme park. The theme park (like all Saunders' theme parks) is failing, the man's child is sick, and his wife is sending him increasingly frantic faxes through the machine hidden in the back of the cave. Furthermore, his cavewoman colleague, Janet, is refusing to stay in character, because she too is having family and financial problems, and is too weary to keep up the charade. The caveman is also being asked to evaluate her performance, every day, by fax – in other words, to betray her. He tells us he is Thinking Positive and Staying Positive, but it is a struggle, and it is a struggle not resolved. We last see him still playing out his caveman role – 'All afternoon we pretend to catch and eat small bugs' – on the off-chance that a visitor will come by. Nobody does.

'Pastoralia' is nearly seventy pages long, allowing Saunders to expand his cast of characters. We get to meet Bradley, Janet's hideous son, who turns up to threaten her with his future, swearing that he will begin 'inadvertently misusing substances' again if she doesn't lend him money. We meet, by fax, Greg Nordstrom, who is under pressure to begin the Staff Remixing, and who needs our caveman to betray Janet.

We also meet Marty and Jeannine, who have been Remixed out of their jobs running the Employees Only shop.

The length of the piece allows Saunders to work with repetition. At the close of every day, the caveman must fax his evaluation of Janet to head office. This becomes the coda to each chapter:

> Do I note any attitudinal difficulties? I do not. How do I rate my Partner overall? Very good. Are there any Situations which require Mediation?
> There are not.
> I fax it in.

When the character finally does betray Janet, this coda changes, and the change ripples right through the story. 'Pastoralia' is Saunders at his best, demonstrating the inextricable link between narrative and rhythm in his work. When I read this collection for the first time I was overwhelmed by a sense of *possibility*. I would never write like Saunders – one has to be content with one's limits, one's style, apparently imposed from without – but reading him always makes me feel how *spacious* art can be. How free it is to be a writer.

In the same year that he published *Pastoralia*, Saunders published a children's book, *The Very Persistent Gappers of Frip*. It tells the story of a girl named Capable who is ground down by her 24-hour job brushing gappers (small, prickly, spherical creatures that scream) from the backs of her goats. Gappers love goats, and when you brush them off and throw them into the sea, it will only be a few hours before they have inched along the seabed and up the steep cliffs of Frip, across the paddocks, and onto the backs of the goats, whose milk is the town's only source of income. Goats won't produce milk if they are covered in screaming gappers. Capable wins against the odds, just as she should – odds that include a useless father, a dead mother, and a set of horrible neighbours – and *The Very Persistent Gappers of Frip*, which is both funny and madly inventive, is that rare thing: a children's book written by an author of books for adults that satisfies both audiences.

What we begin to see in *The Very Persistent Gappers of Frip* is a determined hopefulness in Saunders' work: the weak begin to have the smallest of inklings about their own agency. We start to see more of Saunders' characters winning against the odds. These victories are not always as obvious as Capable's, but they generally involve characters finding a kind of inner strength, or seeing the positive in their lives. Most importantly, they successfully articulate this to themselves. This is exemplified in the character of the grandfather in 'My Flamboyant Grandson', from *In Persuasion Nation*. The unnamed grandfather sins against state power by removing his shoes, which have in-built Everly Strips, designed to receive mandatory advertising from the Everly Readers running along every sidewalk. His shoes are hurting his feet, and he and his isolated, theatrical, 'flamboyant' grandson are late for a Broadway show. The story finishes after the show, which has changed the grandson's life, and after the grandfather has willingly undergone disciplining for removing his Everly Strips: a session in which he is forced to repeatedly Celebrate his Preferences. He finishes by saying to us, about his grandson:

> He looks like no one else, acts like no one else, his clothes are increasingly like plumage, late at night he choreographs using plastic Army men, he fits no mold and has no friends, but I believe in my heart that someday something beautiful may come from him.

The short story is about form – less so than the poem, but more so than the novel. Endings should be fundamental. Their job is not so much resolution; a short-story ending wants to somehow emphasise or echo the quality of the story, as though a story's voice, in its dying fall, can remind us of everything we have just read. Even an airy, apparently open ending, like those in the stories of Lydia Davis or Alice Munro, is a way of saying 'this is what my story is about'.

Saunders' stories often say *my story is about hope* or *my story is about goodness*. And why not? Saunders is a self-described optimist, and there is real pleasure to be had in his empathy and optimism for his unfortunate characters.

But it is possible to see this manoeuvre in Saunders' work as technically limiting. In 'Home', from *Tenth of December*, a young man comes back from either Iraq or Afghanistan to the miserable chaos he created before he left. He is now suffering from war trauma, as well as a horrible childhood and a broken marriage. As he approaches his family, standing terrified on a porch, 'The contours of the coming disaster expanded to include the deaths of all present.' Brilliant, and very scary. But then he gives way, the contours shrink to include only his own disaster, his own unhappy collapse. The family is saved. This is absolutely possible, and very heartening to read. But if it happens this way too many times we start to feel suspicious, a little manipulated.

An example of this triumph of formal convenience over reality comes at the end of 'Christmas', an autobiographical story from *In Persuasion Nation*. It is about the time Saunders spent living in his aunt and uncle's basement and making a very small amount of money as a very incompetent roofer. Saunders calmly and compassionately describes the men he worked with, particularly John, a father of fourteen children, who silently suffers racial taunts and cruelty from those who employ him. In the final scene, all the men, including Saunders, gather for a Christmas party, bringing out their Christmas pay and bonuses to gamble with. Rick, the foulest of them all, gradually wins all of John's money from him. No presents, then, for John's wife or his fourteen children. Saunders finishes: 'I . . . was once a joke of a roofer, a joke of a roofer so beat down he stood by watching as a nice man got cheated out of his Christmas.'

Well, yes, I want to say – but then, no. It isn't my business to know the truth of this situation or to judge its protagonist. But I can see here where the need to end on a note of resolution has forced Saunders into a judgement about his own moral cowardice that closes down other narrative possibilities. The exigencies of narrative, the kind of pressure exerted on all those who would write, demand that we end somewhere, and this ending seems neat enough. But this particular ending does not do everything that Saunders can and does do in stories like 'Sea Oak' and 'Pastoralia', in which you feel the story somehow extending beyond the ending, as though you've had a privileged glimpse into a life that will go on whether you are there or not.

Anyone who has written knows the feeling of the hand behind the back, forcing your story in a particular direction. Saunders' writing shows signs of this; once we have noticed it, it is possible to feel his stories locking into place after a few paragraphs. Not all of them succumb to this pressure, and *Tenth of December* contains some of his best work.

But still, it feels as though there is somewhere *else* George Saunders' stories could go – that there is some unchallenged assumption he has, some unmined psychic difficulty, that could provide a new vein of narrative, a new impulse for his work. His apparently limitless powers of invention don't always extend beyond this narrative of 'hope' or 'goodness'.

After this collection I found myself wishing that he would choose the road less travelled; that he might frighten himself with the psychological possibilities of the situations he sets up.

In 2017 I was given the chance to meet Saunders, chairing a panel at the Sydney Writers' Festival that consisted of him and two other, almost comically different short story writers. You can imagine how I felt. I had already chaired sessions with Jonathan Franzen (an experience so terrifying to contemplate – Franzen is notorious for being impossible to interview – that I thought I might faint as I walked down towards the Roslyn Packer Theatre, my heart unleashing ribbons of beats that I could feel in my head, my legs), James Wood and Helen Garner, people whose work meant as much to me as any real, human relationship. But experience did not make it easier.

As I'd rather suspected he would be, Saunders was about the nicest person I'd ever met. Only met: I didn't spend any length of time with him, didn't become friends with him, although he was immensely friendly. As we sat on stage, watching the crowd file in, I pointed out my father in his front-row seat. Saunders immediately waved at him, and on receiving a wave in return, jerked his thumb at me and called to Dad, 'Good kid!' (This, when I was forty-eight!) As the session opened, he swivelled his body around to face the two other writers, both women. When they spoke, he leaned forward, chin on hand, concentrating hard. If asked a question, he deferred to them first. Even at the time, my heart beating in my head, he made me think irresistibly of the two Canadian farmers in 'Sea Oak' who, on meeting the main characters when they have a flat tyre, insist 'on fixing it, then springing for dinner, then starting a college fund for the babies'.

He willingly signed my beaten-up copy of *Pastoralia*, for me and for Russell. Later, I looked at the front page: 'To Tegan and Michael. Thanks for teaching these!' Even the most generous of practising Buddhists cannot be present in every moment.

Previous to 2017, Saunders was under-read in Australia. He'd never been here, and while he wasn't entirely unknown, it was still possible to spend a day asking people if they'd read him and find that none had – or only those you'd excitedly pressed his books on. However, a review of Saunders in an American publication carried the tacit understanding that the writer was some kind of genius, evinced not just by the astonishing originality of his prose and his numerous awards, including an actual 'Genius Grant' – a MacArthur Fellowship, also awarded to his friend David Foster Wallace – but by the mixture of love and awe he inspired in his fellow writers. Jonathan Franzen said he 'makes the all-but-impossible look effortless', Lorrie Moore that 'there is no one like him', and Wallace himself is recorded as 'standing in the hall [of *Harper's* magazine offices] in his untied high-tops, saying that George Saunders was the most exciting writer in America'.

When we met, Saunders had not yet won the Man Booker with his first novel, *Lincoln in the Bardo*. But there were enough people at the session to tell me what I already knew: that *Lincoln in the Bardo* was going to bring Saunders to a much, much wider audience. The novel was unlike any other published in 2017, and not much like any other novel ever published. Like the cartographers who create maps the size of the countries they represent in the Borges story 'Exactitude in Science', one needs a novel's worth of words to do it justice.

The conceit is this: the son of Abraham Lincoln, Willie, has died and is in a crypt in a graveyard in Washington. In the two or three days following his death, Lincoln comes several times to the graveyard, slides the coffin from the crypt, and holds the boy in his arms. This actually happened.

The characters in the novel are the dead souls who inhabit the graveyard, and Willie is now one of them. However, each of the characters has a problem, which will become the novel's driving concern: they do not know, or will not accept, that they are dead. They are in a fictionalised version of the Tibetan bardo, a middle world where consciousness lingers after death, not having yet fled to its new form – hence the book's dreadful title.

None of this, though, is directly explained in the prose itself. All Saunders' stories begin where stories should – with a voice – but the owner of this voice is generally in conversation with themselves, and not with us. Don't expect exposition, scene-setting, or a list of key characters. It's as though, sitting on a bus, or in a graveyard, or walking through the offices of a minor corporation, we can suddenly hear the inner voices of the people around us. They are all attempting to rewrite their lives, to narrate a self more interesting, more attractive, more able than the one they are stuck with. Sometimes they chant mantras borrowed from charlatan self-help gurus, or get through difficult situations by practising their 'Hatred Abatement Breathing'.

Lincoln in the Bardo opens with the voice of Hans Vollman, a nineteenth-century man, talking about his late marriage to a much younger woman, who was not unnaturally terrified of their wedding night. Seeing her terror, Vollman promised he would keep his distance. They would be friends only, and no-one would be the wiser. His gentleness and generosity were rewarded – after a time his young wife left him a note suggesting that they 'expand the frontiers of our happiness'. Vollman was thrilled; longing for their meeting in bed, he went to work in his printing shop in a state of exalted anticipation. But alas (and here the voice begins to fragment):

A beam from the ceiling came down, hitting me just *here* ... and so our plan must be deferred, while I recovered. Per the advice of my physician, I took to my – A sort of sick-box was judged – was judged to be –

And here the interjection of another voice:

Efficacious.
     roger bevins iii

Efficacious, yes. Thank you, friend.
     hans vollman

This is our introduction – to the central idea of the story; to the story's style, which is much like the script of a play, spoken largely in the voices of these two characters; and to its very particular language. The 'sick-box' isn't for the sick but for the dead – it's a coffin. But each of the people we meet in the graveyard is someone who has chosen to reject this. They are only waiting to recover, so that they can return to their lives and their families. Just as with the characters in Saunders' short stories, their every speech is given in an effort to convince themselves of a more comfortable fiction.

Willie Lincoln died of typhoid, in circumstances terrible for his parents, Abraham and Mary. The night of his death, a long-planned reception was held in the White House. The Lincolns came and went, visiting Willie's sickbed and then assuming party manners for the hundreds of people downstairs. Exposition becomes necessary here, for Hans Vollman and Roger Bevins III can't be expected to know this; they've been dead some time, they don't know the name of the current president, and they're yet to meet Willie. Nor do they know that the Civil War is raging, and that its outcome is uncertain. Saunders solves this puzzle by composing chapters that are made from fragments of other texts; in most cases real books, like the famous *Thirty Years a Slave* by Elizabeth Keckley, who was Mary Todd Lincoln's dresser and close friend. These patchwork chapters first impress as another example of Saunders' ceaseless invention: posed a problem, the author rises to solve it with yet another formal innovation.

But as the novel goes on, and these expositional chapters contain more and longer fragments that we know (after careful googling) to be inventions of the author's, this device becomes a hindrance to Saunders' style, slowing him down. It makes the book feel just slightly mechanical, deliberate where the rest of Saunders' work feels brilliantly involuntary.

Chapter four opens in the voice of Roger Bevins III, who, we learn, had a 'certain predilection', and who, after a rejection from his one-time lover Gilbert, decided to kill himself. However, with wrists slashed, and blood everywhere, he realised that life was in fact beautiful, a 'grand marketplace lovingly stocked with every sublime thing'. He staggered down to the kitchen to find help, and thinks he is there still, waiting to be saved by a servant. In fact he has bled to death. Meanwhile the beautiful multiplicity of life continues to manifest in his speech:

a sleeping dog dream-kicking in a tree-shade triangle;
a sugar pyramid upon a blackwood tabletop being
rearranged grain-by-grain by an indiscernible draft

This multiplicity also manifests in his form – Willie
Lincoln, just arrived, sees:

several sets of eyes   All darting to and fro   All sniffing
His hands (he had multiple sets of hands or else his
hands were so quick they seemed to be many) struck
this way and that, picking things up, bringing them to
his face with a most inquisitive
Little bit scary

willie lincoln

The rules of this invented world require that a child does
not stay in the bardo; as Roger Bevins III puts it, 'These
young ones are not meant to tarry.' But Willie insists that he
has to wait – he feels it – and then we meet Abraham Lincoln
himself, who comes to the crypt, takes Willie's coffin from its
place, and holds his son in his arms. Poor Willie is frantic.
He tries to show his father that he is *here*, not in his body,
and he stands next to him, 'uttering many urgent entreaties
for his father to look *his* way, fuss over and pat *him*'. Finally
he enters Lincoln's body and is able to feel his father's grief.

In the following chapters the central narrative begins to
come together. There's a new happiness amongst the dead

souls, who feel recognised at last – all have been left behind by their living, but here is a living person who has come to see them. They begin to gather around Lincoln, bringing their multitude of stories with them. Dead slaves begin to make an appearance, animating the plot and the material further, passing through Lincoln and feeling his commitment to their liberation. Lincoln begins to shift from real person to central metaphor – he starts to function, literally and figuratively, as a vessel for these neglected people and their stories.

The great pleasure to be had in reading this novel is embodied in the character of Roger Bevins III, ceaselessly reproducing his sensory organs in order to experience more of the world. Saunders himself seems able to see and feel everything and everyone – and each character in *Lincoln in the Bardo*, however small their part, rises off the page fully formed, speaking in a voice that sounds immediately authentic. Here is Saunders' astoundingly tuned ear at work. One of the novel's walk-on characters is a white woman who, in dying, has had to leave her three daughters with a boorish, thoughtless husband. They need her:

Cathryn is soon to begin school. Who will make sure her clothes are correct? Maribeth has a bad foot and is self-conscious and often comes home in tears. To whom will she cry? Alice is nervous, for she has submitted a poem. It is not a very good poem.

Another is Litzie, a slave, who cannot speak, but shakes, and whose story is narrated by her companions:

What was done to her was done to her many times, by many . . . what was done to her was done by big men, small men, boss men, men who happened to be passing the field in which she worked, the teen sons of the boss man or of the men who happened to be passing, a trio of men on a bender who spilled out of the house and, just before departing, saw her there chopping wood . . . what was done to her was: whatever anyone wished to do, and even if someone wished only slightly to do something to her, well, one could do it, it could be done, one did it, it was done and done and –

In Saunders' story collections the authenticity of these voices is the moral work of fiction. Here there is no heavy ethical lifting, no neatly turned conclusion or lesson – there doesn't need to be. The best of his short stories enact their own morality. Just hearing these unheard people speak changes you forever. But a novel wants something more; it yearns towards metaphor; it cannot live on voice alone. Saunders is too good an artist not to know this, and he works diligently to make his Lincoln stand for something. But this effort undoes what he does best. The dead souls who skim around Lincoln, feverishly telling and retelling their stories, are the ones truly alive – and the single living character feels, if not dead, half asleep.

Saunders forgets that Lincoln is just another person. He stuffs him with novelistic responsibility. And again, it feels deliberate, where in Saunders' other work this effort is invisible.

If ever a country needed a metaphor, America is it, and *Lincoln in the Bardo*, with its towering, sombre stand-in for all that yearns towards decency in American life, provides just that. Containing multitudes, Lincoln manages to embody a united people at a time when the country seems in a million little pieces. Because of this, and its author's astounding powers of invention, *Lincoln in the Bardo* is a novel that will and should be celebrated. You can't compare George Saunders to other writers – he is doing something riskier, more exciting, and finally more meaningful. It's only if you compare George Saunders to himself that *Lincoln in the Bardo* disappoints – just a little.

If you are a reader like I am you will have become closely acquainted with more than one body of work. There's something particular in the reading of one author's entire oeuvre. Easy with Austen; less so with Dickens. I have read every book written by Jane Austen, Tim Winton, Helen Garner, David Malouf, Charlotte Wood, Jonathan Franzen, Kazuo Ishiguro, Alice Munro, James Wood, Alan Hollinghurst and George Saunders. In this way you enter into a lifelong conversation with the author. You watch their material change, their attitudes to it shifting. You learn *how* to read them. Tim Winton has said of Munro that she has 'trained the reader – and the editors of most significant US magazines – to read her as Alice Munro. A bigger achievement than it first seems.' This training is possible with any writer, if you love them enough. And by this I do mean them, not just the work. Through long acquaintance with their writing and, in my case, natural curiosity about the person themselves, you feel you begin to understand what they want, what they are trying to do. As with old friends, you forgive their bad days, their misconceived ideas. It's inevitable that you won't always think their efforts successful.

George Saunders' writing has its limits. But those limits are staked so far beyond everyone else's. There he is, right at the edge of the cliff, the wind blasting around him, joyfully at work. How exciting it is to be alive at the same time as this remarkable writer.

Georgia Blain

In October 2015 I walked up to a cafe in Leura to meet my friend Georgia Blain. She was in the mountains for the weekend and had texted me to see if we might catch up. It was the same as all of our meetings: Georgia was there before I was and had already ordered something to drink. She gave me a big grin as I sat down and off we went, making no small talk. Our subjects were these: our children, most particularly our teenage daughters, as this was common ground; our writing; what we were reading; our mothers. My own mother had died more than a year earlier – Georgia was in the process of moving hers, the writer and broadcaster Anne Deveson, into a nursing home. Anne had Alzheimer's, and it had become impossible to look after her in her own house.

On this particular day Georgia steered us towards what was understandably preoccupying her. She had two pieces of news. First, she'd finished her latest novel, *Between a Wolf and a Dog*. It was about a woman who has a brain tumour. The main character, a mother of two grown-up daughters, chooses to end her own life, rather than let the cancer end it.

The second piece of news was that Georgia had just learned that the writer Rosie Scott, her closest friend, her first reader and second mother, had been diagnosed with an aggressive brain tumour.

It was hard to believe. There was so much to process. Grief, which Georgia was already too familiar with. Shock at the coincidence. And then the painful dilemma. The book was due out in six months. What should she do?

I'm speeding across the surface of this long, complex conversation, in which we circled the problem, always returning to Georgia's devotion to Rosie and fear of hurting her. We drank our coffee. People came and went from the tables around us. And we reached the decision I'm sure Georgia had already reached without me – that she should go forward. The book was written. It would be published. Georgia was not sure what she would say to Rosie.

The rest has become common knowledge to Australian readers. A month after this, Georgia herself had a seizure in her backyard in Marrickville. In hospital, she had brain

surgery and was given a diagnosis: glioblastoma, the same
tumour that Rosie had. It was not a story that made any
sense; it had already used up all its right to drama. As
Georgia wrote, 'If this were fiction, I would say it was too
far-fetched.'

The last time I saw Georgia was after lunch with our friend
Charlotte Wood. The car was full of the quiet sounds of
two people settling themselves; clicking our seatbelts,
Georgia pulling her bag onto her lap, me turning the key in
the ignition, putting the windows down. We were talking
about writing, and Georgia said, 'These days, I think it's
just about telling a story.'

'Like Rosie's work,' I said. 'When I started reading her,
it felt like I started to notice stories. How nice it was to be
told a story.'

'Exactly. She's modest,' added Georgia as we drove up
Juliett Street. 'She just wants to stay in print.'

These are painful words to write because they recall so
vividly the feel of those days – bright and clear, warming up
for a terrible summer that Georgia wouldn't have to endure.
The conversation with Charlotte at the cafe was still in
the air around us, the talk about our work, other writers,
people and their folly, our husbands and our children, and
Georgia's impending death. You knew not to be a chicken
when you were with Georgia, because she was one of the
bravest people you'd ever meet. You knew what she was

facing, and that any terror or discomfort on your own part had to be overcome in order to make the space for Georgia to say whatever she needed to say.

Georgia died thirteen months after her diagnosis. In those thirteen months, after the operation, during chemotherapy and radiation, and in the very brief respite she had from treatment, she wrote almost continuously. After the publication of *Between a Wolf and a Dog* came her series of columns for *The Saturday Paper*, 'The Unwelcome Guest', and then her last book, *The Museum of Words*.

Rereading *Between a Wolf and a Dog*, I'm returned immediately to the two of us in the car, talking – that simple, corporeal there-ness that becomes so hard to let go of when a friend dies. And of course I'm returned to the idea of story. I'm sorry to say that the first time I read *Between a Wolf and a Dog* I did so too quickly, my eyes sped along the lines by grief and fear at what I would find. I was a chicken. I couldn't take it in properly. I knew too much about it.

But now I can read it for pleasure. Of course the people in *Between a Wolf and a Dog* are all suffering in some way. It's not just Hilary, who has a brain tumour and has to make a choice between letting it kill her or killing herself; there's Ester and Lawrence, whose marriage has broken up; there's April, Ester's sister, who has committed a crime against sisterhood that can't be forgiven; and there are

Ester's clients in her psychotherapy practice, all fighting their way through unhappiness. It's in many ways a sad book. But sadness is not the point. This is a story. You really want to know what happens, and you can feel the riddle of each character moving closer to solution as you read. The book brings you deep satisfaction as well as tears. It's the work of someone who's spent a lifetime writing fiction.

The Museum of Words is different. A short book. Not a memoir of dying, although it is about illness and treatment, and the impossibility of leaving loved people behind. It moves between its subjects, using the writer's illness reflexively, leading into description of the things most important to her. In this way the book is about language and its function in a writer's life. It's about Anne Deveson, and growing up with a writer as a mother. It's about Rosie Scott, whom Georgia met through Anne, and her importance to their family. Georgia describes fights with Anne, ending with the two of them rushing to be the first to tell Rosie – hearing the engaged signal on Rosie's line let her know that Anne had got there first. The book is also about Andrew, Georgia's partner, and Odessa, their daughter.

This is a book with spaces in it. Georgia wrote relatively spare prose, drifting only occasionally into the kind of lush description that opens *Between a Wolf and a Dog*. In *The Museum of Words* the spareness feels less willed. I had the sense as I read of the writer on the spine of a bare hill, making her way carefully across a sentence with the concentration of someone who might lose her balance and has nowhere to fall. Georgia's editor at Scribe, Marika Webb-Pullman, says the decision to leave in some of these spaces was deliberate. A book should enact its subject matter. There is of course something beyond story – otherwise, why write, why not just tell? The art is in the form.

Webb-Pullman and Georgia's husband, the photographer and filmmaker Andrew Taylor, have been sensitive editors, allowing Georgia's words, which describe loss of language, to also demonstrate it. One feels a meticulous effort to preserve the original.

The book has some of its spaces filled by photographs. Many of these were taken by Andrew: portraits of Georgia that reveal how luminously beautiful she was, images from the hospital where she received treatment, a final photograph of the carpet of blossoms in the backyard where Georgia collapsed with her first seizure. The impression is of punctuation rather than illustration, as though each image is part of the book's syntax, as in the work of W.G. Sebald or the early novels of Michael Ondaatje.

For anyone who knew Georgia, the effect of reading this book will be filmic – a sequence of Georgia's words and Andrew's images cut with moving pictures of Georgia as she was: statuesque, as though the word had been invented to describe her; laconic (she spoke in a deep drawl that always contained the possibility of laughter); briskly unsentimental.

It is odd to recall that because Georgia did not indulge in sentiment, her company allowed feeling to expand. You felt you could say anything to her, and she to you. Her first book of nonfiction, *Births Deaths Marriages* (2008), was an open conversation with her readers about some of the most intimate experiences of her life; *The Museum of Words* continues that exchange.

Perhaps my favourite sequences, because they dwell on Georgia's most beloved subject, describe Odessa. Georgia was always cautious about including Odessa in her writing, 'wary about reducing [her] to words'. But in showing Odessa making her way through the study of two languages – French and Latin – by looking carefully at her daughter at work, she doesn't expose her but respects her. She recalls the toddler Odessa's phrase, 'I hope so the blowflowers', but swerves away from talking about loss into talking about language: 'It was the dandelions she was wishing for.' Again, absence – always a feature of Georgia Blain's writing, but at its most powerful here – does its work. In refusing to be sentimental about her daughter, Georgia evokes a terrible grief. Impossible to read these sections without tears.

How to make sense of all this? I find some comfort in two scenes; one, from Andrew Taylor's introduction to the book. The copy-edit of *The Museum of Words* has come back.

Georgia is too tired, too far gone, to work on it. Andrew sits at the kitchen table with his laptop open. Georgia lies on the couch, the TV on, with Odessa by her side. Andrew calls out changes. Georgia responds, or Odessa does, or Andrew makes the change himself.

And this, one of the book's final images: Georgia is visiting Anne in her nursing home. Anne isn't able to retain the fact of Georgia's illness. Because of this, Georgia was denied two things: she couldn't receive comfort from Anne, who didn't understand that her daughter was dying, and she couldn't properly mourn Anne herself. 'I've learnt that the best thing to do is tell her that I love her and sit in silence holding her hand. There is not much more that I can do . . . I know that I have limited time.'

I remember when I first heard the news of Georgia's diagnosis, and the urge to communicate with her was immediate. I sat in the backyard, staring at my phone, wondering what I could possibly say to my friend whose life had been overturned. I remember the awful irresolution of being unable to find the right words, of being unable to generate a narrative that might make sense of this.

Georgia died in December 2016, and Anne three days later. In May 2017, Rosie also died. There is no special reason why these three remarkable women shared so much ill luck, and there is no narrative that will restore order to the utter chaos of life. Perhaps you are next; perhaps I am. What we do have is this: a small family, sitting together;

a daughter holding a mother's hand; and this fine book that looks chaos directly in the face and attempts to record it.

On that day in Juliett Street, after lunch with Charlotte, we'd wound down our talk about writing and we were talking about our thought patterns, the way certain painful ideas could lodge and be difficult to shift. I asked her if anything was preoccupying her at the moment, and she sighed and said, 'No. Just saying goodbye.'

Georgia was pressed by circumstance into these exchanges time and again. She hated false profundity and sentiment, and she would hate it if I pretended that we had shared something very remarkable at this moment. She was only interested in the truth, and would have laughed or snarled at the neatness of this 'final memory' of her. Georgia's writing was about people close up, the truth of an exchange like this one, the inadequate way we are in the face of death.

We kept driving, and talked about Odessa, and Andrew, and *The Museum of Words*. We pulled up at her house. The sun shone, there were new leaves on the trees, her dog – 'the only one in this house who carries on like a pork chop' – barked at me, and she gave me a quick kiss on the cheek. We planned to catch up again soon, and though we wouldn't do that, we texted jokes, banalities, and some messages of love until a few days before she died.

A mole, a viper, a toad

In the Dark Room (2005) is Irish writer Brian Dillon's first book, a memoir of his childhood and early adulthood. Dillon's mother suffered from two lifelong conditions, one of which killed her. She had depression, severe and unremitting, caused in part by her other condition, scleroderma, a disease that comes with a terrible bouquet of symptoms, including thickening and tightening of the skin, as well as other organs and the arteries and veins. As the disease progresses, sufferers of scleroderma find it harder and harder to swallow, to breathe, and finally, to move at all. Their oesophagus comes to resemble, and feel like, 'a glass tube'; the skin of their face, at first as though cosmetically tightened, can begin to show lines and then deep lesions like cuts or slices, known as 'en coup de sabre'. The sufferer can also experience Raynaud's syndrome, in which blood flow to the extremities is stopped. Dillon's mother wore gloves to try to keep her hands warm, but also to hide the fact that her hands were becoming like claws. She died when the author was sixteen, leaving him with his father and two younger brothers in a house enclosed in a constricting silence: 'In the evenings, I retreated to my bedroom. My brothers started to do the same.' The three brothers did not learn from their restrained, reserved father how to manage or even to talk about grief, and they'd learned only unhappiness from their mother, who used to say that she felt her head would explode – whether from the depression or from the literal pressure of her disease isn't entirely clear.

Five years later, Dillon, still living with his father and brothers, is at university. He wakes one morning, having slept late, to see his brother Kevin at his bedroom door. Kevin is saying something about the police. It takes some moments for his meaning to become clear. Their father is dead, after a heart attack in the street, ten minutes from their house. Dillon experiences a kind of disbelief, while his body becomes obedient to the new truth:

> My father is dead. No, my *mother* is dead (I know, because I was here: I lay here, in this room, on this bed, the morning after she died.) But my father is dead too. In a second, I am at the end of the bed, dressing. All I

can think is: what do we do now? What exactly are we *supposed* to do now?

The three boys make arrangements with the undertaker who buried their mother. They return to the house. And now they are alone – alone, but together, until the two younger boys have finished school.

Before publishing *In the Dark Room* Brian Dillon had written essays, criticism, fiction and history. Dillon is the Head of Critical Writing in Art and Design at the Royal College of Art in London; he is the UK editor of *Cabinet* magazine and the essay collection *Ruins* and the author of *Tormented Hope: Nine Hypochondriac Lives* (2009), a study of illness and imagination, which includes such diverse subjects as Andy Warhol and Florence Nightingale, and *The Great Explosion* (2015), a Sebaldian account of an accident at a factory in Kent in the early twentieth century. His latest book, *Essayism*, was published in 2017.

Of course, given this writing history, *In the Dark Room* is no ordinary memoir. It isn't so much about the miseries of his mother's illness, or even about grief – or it is, but it can't quite bear to be. Instead, it is a meditation on space or spaces, on objects, on memory. It attempts what all good books attempt – a kind of lifting off, a swooping away from experience. Great art does this. It does not reproduce misery; it transforms it. It makes company out of loneliness, living flesh from ashes. Any writer knows that when they are writing at their best they leave experience in the dust, as dust.

But how can I put this? I found *In the Dark Room* too depressing. I couldn't tell, I can't tell, whether this was a result of my own late brush with depression (I call it a brush, but that's a trick – I'm trying to trick depression into moving on, leaving me alone) or whether Dillon had failed. He hadn't left experience behind. He had reproduced unhappiness. I couldn't imagine the reader who felt altered for the better by *In the Dark Room*. Afterwards I could only look away, horrified and sorry for its author, and wishing I had not said I would read his books.

Time passed, and other books intervened, and I privately hoped that the editor of the journal I was writing for would forget that I had promised to write about *Essayism*. I looked through my little pile of Dillon's books; they, too, defeated me. *Tormented Lives* seemed to be another anatomy of melancholy, and his novel, *Sanctuary*, began with a description of a woman succumbing to a migraine. Anyone susceptible to migraines knows how easily they can be called into existence – even the word starts a glittering behind my eyes. I had to put the book away from me, but not before noting that it was written in a style so refined you immediately began to imagine it being parodied. I slid the books onto the shelf behind a doorway in our hall, thinking I wouldn't need them. I read, in the meantime, a new book by Joan Silber. I read, for the first time, Svetlana Alexievich, and engaged in an excited email exchange about her work with a writing friend. Then, for reasons I can't recall, I decided to try Proust again.

I'd started *Swann's Way* between five and ten times since my late teens, and every time been defeated by it. Adam Gopnik says, 'Everybody tries to climb Mt. Proust, though many a stiff body is found on the lower slopes, with the other readers stepping over it gingerly.' Mine was one of the bodies that better readers stepped over; it may yet be, as I am still on the first volume of *À la recherche du temps perdu*. I had no real intention of picking myself up and trying again. It was a long train journey that did it – I thought, I'll take *Swann's Way* and nothing else, then I'll have no choice but to read it. I'd had success with this method twenty years earlier, reading *The Man Who Loved Children* on a train between Madrid and Seville.

It was Proust's sentences that defeated me all those other times. In the Moncrieff-Kilmartin translation I'm reading some appear to stretch beyond the reader's vision, their horizon out of reach. I'm sure that's why I used to panic – halfway through a sentence, and unable to see dry land before or behind me, sometimes having to thrash back to recover the sentence's subject. But this time, reading on, the backyards of western Sydney flickering past, I started to see that the syntax of the sentences was imitated in the structure of the book itself. That there was art, not just information, at work. That it might be a long time before I saw dry land again, but that it might not matter. I read about dinner at Combray and the profusion of asparagus on the dinner table; there was so much of it this spring. The tips were pale purple and green, and eating them lent a peculiar fragrance to the chamber pot. I read about Aunt Léonie, who took to her bed when her husband died, and who was maintaining a delicate balance between hoping for a recovery that might allow her to come downstairs and even to sit in the garden, and making sure that everyone knew she was dying and would never see the garden again. I read about Aunt Léonie's maid, Françoise, stumping up and down the stairs with plates of asparagus, which, I later learned, she was serving so frequently not because of the excess of them, but in order to torture the little scullery maid who'd got pregnant out of wedlock and was violently allergic to asparagus. I remember, last time, worrying that I would never be able to retain it all.

But I've finally learned to go limp – to float on my back and wait for the rip to take me the slow way home. Who cares if I can't remember where the Guermantes family live or which church has the hawthorn berries arranged on the altar? The pleasure is in the lostness, the near-drowning in Proust's unbelievable memory and unbelievably beautiful prose. It's experimental writing. I never understood this – I'd never got far enough to be able to see that Proust had invented a whole genre, the piling and piling of sentences that somehow imitated memory itself. And I'd never got far enough to enjoy myself.

In *Essayism* Brian Dillon says that when he became depressed for the second or third time (the only condition he seems to have inherited from his mother) 'once more I could hardly read at all'. Depression was not just the 'drying up of one's reservoir of symbols and figures for a continued and perhaps even improved life', it was a cessation of the ability to *see* 'symbols and figures' in other people's writing. Instead of vistas, a blasted plain; instead of running water, a place where water has never been, nor ever will be. Reading Proust, I am reminded that I am no longer depressed. I lie in bed laughing at the abundance, at the profusion of meanings and images – and laughing at the joyful contemporaneity of reading, allowing me to live alongside Proust, see what he sees, feel what he feels.

And reading him is not just joyful but fertile – the bee of my mind buzzes up, laden with pollen, and back to Brian Dillon's *Tormented Lives*, to read his chapter on Marcel Proust, who took to his bed just as Aunt Léonie did, but very much more productively. Reading this, and finding life in it, I think perhaps I am ready for *Essayism* after all.

Essayism is what Martin Amis might describe as a 'slim vol.' – it's a small, beautiful book with an austerely embossed cover and deep gutters around its dense interior text. It did give me a small shiver of horror on approach: there is an asceticism to Dillon's style (his whole style, I mean, each one of his books, the chilly grip he has on his subject matter, even the look of him in photographs, tall and skinny and white as soap) that could not be more different from Proust's hilarious luxuriance. But here I came to understand that I had not been reading Dillon properly – that previously our meeting as writer and reader had been a meeting of two undertakers, our handshake mutually cold, signifying our agreement that things could never improve. And that perhaps at least one of us needed to be happy for our exchange to be fruitful.

What is *Essayism*? Its writer admits that he has 'no clue how to write about the essay as a stable entity or established class, how to trace its history diligently from uncertain origins through successive phases of literary dominance' – and praise be for that. The book is instead a series of attempts – of essays, of course – at delineating or describing the form. Each chapter is a few pages, beginning with an idea: 'On essays and essayists', 'On origins', 'On lists', and as the book begins to become something else, 'On consolation'. The book is also a story of the book being written, and of Dillon going under entirely. 'Each day,' he tells us early on,

> I sat at my desk in an office at the end of the garden, and cried and smoked and tried to write – tried to write this book – and each day finally gave myself up to fantasies of suicide. I would walk out of this suburb along country lanes to a secluded stretch of railway line and lay my head on the track in the moonlight.

There is an almost tidal pull towards suicide in Dillon, and *Essayism* is a story of resisting it. In some chapters he evokes the feeling of being frozen at the moment of it, not quite falling, not quite dead, a character swinging cartoon-like in midair beyond a cliff's edge. He continues working, producing reams of freelance criticism and even another book, telling his psychiatrist that his thoughts of suicide are receding, when 'in fact I had been sitting down to work each day for years with the conviction that I must kill myself, soon'. But it would be wrong to suggest that these thoughts and this narrative dominate the book. There is a modesty, a spareness, a total moral restraint in the way Dillon tells his unhappiness. And what is more – or in fact, because of this – there is art.

Each chapter of this book contains meditations on the work of another writer, or of many other writers. There is a lesson here about reading, and how deep reading informs the way we think and the way we narrate ourselves. Dillon notices himself using the word 'parsing', an expression he first read in an article by the music writer Ian Penman in 1997: 'It was as though I thought life were something that needed to be defused like a bomb or parsed like an algebraic equation before it could be lived.' He quotes this line and asks himself, 'how many times ... have I stolen that last phrase in print, or let it pass through my mind as a judgment on myself or others?' He instinctively understands what literature can be for many of us – a way of thinking about ourselves, of describing ourselves to ourselves. In an aside on Henry James and his (hardly unique) inability to write well about sex, he tells us that even that most particular and precise of novelists can 'end up adverting to a character's "hard manhood" when that is not what he meant at all'. Hear that lovely echo of Eliot, like a bell ringing at the end of a street, muffled by distance and habitation.

There are many passages in the book that both describe the work of another writer and then somehow enact it, play it out. Most remarkable of these is a chapter on melancholy, which begins as an examination of the critic Cyril Connolly and his book *The Unquiet Grave*, published under the pen name Palinurus in 1944. The book is 'an essay, an anthology, a *complaint*'. Dillon reads Connolly with us, expressing surprise that he was able to find a publisher for such an odd collection of fragments and quotations and reflections: a collection, we begin to see, not unlike *Essayism* itself. Dillon notes Connolly's tendency towards the epigram; for instance: 'Today an artist must expect to write on water and cast on sand.' The following chapter, another on consolation, describes Dillon's move to the seaside city of Margate as his life is coming apart. We see him sleeping on a mattress on the floor, smoking in the basement of his apartment building, and riding his bike again and again to the deserted seafront, imagining throwing himself into the water. 'I never left the flat without feeling that I might blow away in the wind that ceaselessly attacked the town.

I would turn into sand or spray.' The reference to Connolly is there, the connection is made, the art reveals itself, but quietly, thoughtfully, without fanfare.

In *Essayism* you will find a list of possible subjects for the essay, drawn from those already written; a list of things the essay might formally be – and might, simultaneously, not be; a story of reading; a collection of closely written passages on sentences, on punctuation; and a frankly curious examination of the obsessions of other writers (such as Thomas Browne, seventeenth-century author of the *Pseudodoxia Epidemica*, who included in his experiments the trapping of a mole, a viper and a toad under the same glass – the mole, as Dillon tells us, prevailed). Perhaps we should let Dillon, describing the form, describe his own book, which

> pursue[s] its adventure by the paradoxical means of an ordered stasis: all its elements arranged as if in a cabinet of curiosities, an elaborate microcosm that freezes in an image some version of the world outside the collection. In this essayistic *Wunderkammer*, things are allowed to be themselves alone, but will inevitably enter into metaphoric relations with each other, essaying lines of analogy or affinity.

Finally, *Essayism* is the story of intense unhappiness and the possibility of happiness. It can't help but speak sometimes of the author's mother and her suffering, and the way she transmitted this to her son. It isn't sentimental; it never tries to pretend that there is a lesson to be learned from this poor woman's misery, and the misery of her poor sons. Perhaps I might not recommend Dillon's books to someone who is similarly prone to the contagion of unhappiness; it takes a certain readerly fortitude to resist the dark reasonings of the memoir, the catalogue of miseries that is *Tormented Lives*. But I was grateful to have been, at last, the right reader for *Essayism*. It is Dillon's life preserver, thrown to himself.

Inventing the teenager

For most of us who care to think about such things, the teenager was invented by J.D. Salinger in 1951. Of course, before he was described in literature, the teenager was a naturally occurring phenomenon in postwar America. As that country became the world's richest, a whole generation of young, mainly white people emerged who did not need to go immediately to work, whose parents' relative wealth and resulting access to inventions like the washing machine and the motor car had created a new leisure. What Holden Caulfield has that young people did not have before him is *time to think*. Like a 1940s Hamlet he wanders the streets of New York, outside the jurisdiction of parents and teachers, free to ponder the phoneys he has known, free to feel miserable, free to feel trapped by the future his parents imagine for him.

Every semester I stand in front of a class of first- or second-year university students and I ask them what books they have read. The answers differ from country to city, from inner to outer west, from degree to degree. Every year fewer of them have read much at all. Once, it was an anomaly to find a creative writing student who had not read many books (how we used to laugh in the staffroom – the thought of taking a creative writing class without being a dedicated reader!); now it is the norm. The anomaly is the student who has read books despite the fact that they have a phone to soothe them and provide continuous company, despite the fact that they don't need to leave the house to see a movie, despite the fact that there is simply so much else to do. I don't despair anymore. I just notice it.

Each year I ask my students if they've read *The Catcher in the Rye*. One of them, two of them, none of them. Then I ask them if they've heard of it. Some have. Then I tell them about it, and the invention of the teenager. I tell them that *The Catcher in the Rye* didn't act the way a book once had, hewing to some kind of narrative order, reasserting particular attitudes as certainties, certainties that were invisible but vital to the cohesion of Western civilisation. Here was a voice that knew nothing for sure, doubted everything, and what was more, told secrets about his experience that had never been told in books before.

Literature begets literature, I tell my students, and *The Catcher in the Rye* wouldn't have been possible without its modernist forebears: Virginia Woolf's *Mrs Dalloway*, James Joyce's *Ulysses*, Joseph Conrad's *Heart of Darkness*. All of these books took as their subject, directly or indirectly, the total collapse of certainty after World War I. If millions of young men could be fed into the newly mechanised maw of world war, a war that started for spurious reasons and continued just as spuriously, what was left to believe in? Modernist literature reflects that fragmenting belief. *The Catcher in the Rye*, written after its author served in World War II, simply carried on the fragmenting.

Of course, before Holden Caulfield, there were other teenagers in literature. Not just young people – actual, rebellious teenagers, fizzing with seditious ingenuity. Think Lydia Bennet in *Pride and Prejudice*. Or Jane Eyre, fighting her way out of the Reed family and her horrible school, or Heathcliff and Cathy, spurning moderation in pursuit of their violent love. But three lesser-known literary teenagers were the ones who spoke most directly to me when I was young.

'In the summer all right-minded boys built huts in the furze-hill behind the College'. This is the first clause of the first sentence of *Stalky & Co*, Rudyard Kipling's 1899 book about his years at the United Services College in the unusually named little seaside village of Westward Ho! in Devon. Kipling, born in 1865, began his schooling there in 1878.

Stalky & Co was originally published as separate pieces in journals such as *Windsor Magazine* and *McClure's Magazine*. The 'Stalky' of the title is Arthur Corkran, one of a triumvirate made up of Beetle, Kipling's alter ego; M'Turk (or Turkey), based on Kipling's schoolfriend George Beresford; and Stalky himself, based on their friend Lionel Dunsterville, who became a major-general in the British Army. Stalky, Beetle and M'Turk share a study – Number Five – one of the privileges of the older boys in a school like the College, or Coll., as the boys call it. Here, Beetle writes poetry, M'Turk reads about art and architecture and puts up stencils and pictures on the walls, and Stalky, the general-to-be, directs operations.

The plot runs thus: Stalky, Beetle and M'Turk are bent on escaping a day of compulsory sport with the rest of the Coll. Their aim is the hut they've hollowed out in the furze that covers the cliffs, looking westwards to the sea. As the book opens they learn that their hut has been discovered and destroyed. Lesser boys would have given in and gone down to cricket as requested, but these boys are endlessly inventive. Stalky quickly enrols them in the Natural History Society, whose boundaries are broader than the rest of the students', and the boys set out through the undergrowth to an eyrie at the cliffs' edge. They bring out their books, they make themselves comfortable and, hidden from the rest of the world, they read. 'The sea snored and gurgled; the birds, scattered for the moment by these new animals, returned to their businesses, and the boys read on in the rich, sleepy silence.'

Each chapter swirls over a half-hidden reef of books. Books for Stalky & Co are an escape from the absurd world of their military college, its rules and rewards, its insistence on a manacled future, its focus on right-minded boys with 'pure souls'. Books are rebellion, utter subversion. Stalky, the most conservative of the three, reads Surtees' *Jorrocks' Jaunts and Jollities*, a series of comic novels about a sporting cockney grocer, originally serialised in *New Sporting Magazine*. Beetle, as Stalky proclaims to their friends, 'reads an ass called Brownin', and M'Turk reads an ass called Ruskin' – author of the famous *Fors Clavigera*, a collection of treatises written for working men about the moral value of art and work. Stalky, Beetle and M'Turk read books the way I was reading as a teenager: in an unarticulated search for like minds, for company.

The boys return to their eyrie again and again, sometimes cheekily strolling out right under the noses of Mr King, their loathed Latin teacher, and Mr Prout, their housemaster. Finally, King and Prout follow them. What the masters don't know is that the boys have befriended Colonel Dabney, the landowner, and have been expressly invited to range over his land as much as they wish. Triumph: King and Prout are found crossing Colonel Dabney's land and are apprehended by the game-keeper, who holds them at gunpoint until Colonel Dabney appears. And there the two masters are given a dressing-down for trespassing, the very crime they were hoping to convict the boys of, all within earshot of the evil three, who by this time are hidden in the gamekeeper's parlour, lying on the rugs and the couch and crying with laughter.

Back at school the three boys, still showing the effects of an hour's helpless laughter, are called up to the headmaster for trespassing and for public drunkenness. They cite their membership of the Natural History Society and produce a badger given to them by the gamekeeper's wife as proof of their commitment. Then they explain the truth of the matter, which they've withheld from King and Prout, to their headmaster, and he, understanding them utterly, perpetrates the 'howling injustice' of caning them all. He finishes by giving them a pile of new books, and the boys return to Number Five, exultant.

When *Stalky & Co* was published the reviews were mixed. 'An unpleasant book about unpleasant boys at an unpleasant school,' said one. Somerset Maugham and H.G. Wells were among those who weighed in on its nastiness, and the 'odiousness' of its main characters. Unhealthy, unboylike, the demonic inventions of 'the spoiled child of an utterly brutalised public', Stalky, Beetle and M'Turk were 'three small fiends in human likeness'.

In other words, they were teenagers. These three fifteen-year-olds methodically, brilliantly undermined everything that readers thought they knew about the public school. This was not *Tom Brown's School Days* or *The Fifth Form at*

St Dominic's, or even *Eric, or Little by Little*. This was *The Breakfast Club*, only these characters, almost permanently on detention, had brains and education, and they used these to defeat cant, brutality and sycophancy in all its forms. When I was fifteen I knew no-one who spoke my language so clearly as these three nineteenth-century schoolboys. They were the best companions I ever had.

I'm the mother of two teenagers now. They're both readers, particularly my daughter. In my son's case, this is partly to do with access to his computer and phone. When he's asked to take a break from these he generally ends up reading. My daughter – and I think this is to do with both her personality and her gender – reads to relax, for company, for entertainment. Every so often I try to nudge one or the other of them towards a certain book. Look, I'll tell you – sometimes I *pay* them to read books. Our kids don't get pocket money, but they do get paid for work around the house. In this way I paid Alice to read *Pride and Prejudice*. I also paid for *In Cold Blood*. I paid my son to read *The Wolves of Willoughby Chase* a few years ago. Most recently I paid my daughter to read *The Catcher in the Rye*.

She'd started it a few times because I kept pressing it on her, telling her about its importance, its place as a pivot in English literature, the way it invented teenagehood. But every time Alice picked it up she was put off. 'He's so *annoying*,' she kept saying. 'I hate the sound of his voice.'

Sometimes in my classes I do a kind of dramatic clutching of the heart when my students tell me they haven't read the books I'm talking about. I try to avoid the dramatic clutching with Alice, but I feel it. I wanted to clutch my heart dramatically when she said that Holden Caulfield was annoying. Finally, though, curious or needing the money, she read it, all the way through. I'm sure she has some private responses to it that I won't press her for, but her general response was twofold – first, he continued to be really annoying; second, it was *so sad.*

It never would have occurred to me to use the word 'sad' about Holden's experience. But of course Alice is right – it *is* sad. He's all on his own out there. He is absolutely lost, lost in his own city. The future terrifies him and nobody knows or cares what he is feeling. You can imagine his parents – 'grand people' – going to meeting after meeting with various school principals, working, not to help Holden, but to assure each new principal that at *this* school he'll shape up, become like all the right-minded boys. What a cold reader I was. I knew Holden was speaking for me but I didn't think about him with any tenderness.

This is partly because he didn't think this way about himself either. Empathy has been refined and improved in the new millennium. My millennial children exist in a much more empathetic atmosphere than Holden Caulfield did, in a place where theirs and their friends' feelings are noticed, valued. But don't forget that this has a lot to do with their worth as consumers. In the current economy, what teenagers care about matters, and so they see themselves reflected in every surface. You really know you exist when someone tries to sell you something.

Some years ago I asked a literature class, 'What happened in 1939?'

Total silence. This time I didn't clutch my heart. Instead, I started for the door, saying, 'If someone can't tell me what happened in 1939, I'm leaving.' We all laughed; I wouldn't have left, but it's good to create a bit of comic tension in a classroom. Then someone shouted, 'World War Three!'

I grabbed the door handle and swung round to glare at the class.

'I mean World War Two!' shouted the same panicked student, and I let go of the door. We laughed again. We returned to the novel we were studying.

A book that both my children read voluntarily – and then saw the movie, and then read the book again – is Suzanne Collins' *The Hunger Games*. The plot is simple: the heroine, Katniss Everdeen, lives in a dystopian future where a group of lower class children and teenagers are 'reaped' – randomly selected once a year to fight to the death in a huge arena, all of it televised.

The Hunger Games is written in the strangely affectless prose that seems to dominate YA writing these days. I'm looking now at its opening sentences:

> When I wake up, the other side of the bed is cold. My fingers stretch out, seeking Prim's warmth but finding only the rough canvas cover of the mattress. She must have had bad dreams and climbed in with our mother. Of course she did. This is the day of the reaping.

There doesn't seem to be anything either terrible or wonderful about this writing. It is almost wholly uninflected. There are a lot of short sentences, heightening the sense that this girl has little time to tell you what she needs to tell you. The descriptions are adequate. The plotting is solid. Despite the fact that *The Hunger Games* owes its existence, in part, to the literature that came before (to George Orwell's *1984*, and to Shirley Jackson's terrifying short story 'The Lottery' (1948), set in a village that gathers once a year to choose a person to stone to death), the writing itself does not seem to know this. It is almost entirely textureless.

Still. Last year, teaching creative writing at a city university, I found myself talking about *The Hunger Games* to my class. I had been trying to explain to my students why some narratives have traction in a culture. *The Catcher in the Rye* had traction because the teenager was coming into being and Salinger happened to be there to name him at exactly the right moment. The moment was not right for the characters of *Stalky & Co*, which remains a little-read book amongst Kipling's enormous oeuvre. Trying to think of a text that might make sense to them, I suggested that the reason *The Hunger Games* had been so popular was because it spoke to something unexpressed in teenagers' hearts. It describes without seeming to their sense that they are being forced out into a world they did not choose and did not create. The characters' struggle to survive, the way they are forced to attack one another in order to live, and the way this seems to have been invented for the amusement of adults: this is what it feels like to be young today.

I said these things wondering if they would have any effect. But as I looked around the room, every teenager in front of me was nodding. Briefly, warmly, we occupied the same space.

I recently read two books by the 2015 Nobel Prize winner, Svetlana Alexievich. Originally from Belarus, Alexievich has spent years travelling around Russia interviewing ordinary Russians for what she sometimes describes as 'chorus novels'. Instead of trying to tell stories, she asks questions and records answers, with little or no descriptive intervention. The result is powerful. While *Voices from Chernobyl* is the more instantly arresting book (its opening monologue by the wife of one of the first firemen on the scene after the reactor exploded is horrible, riveting), *Secondhand Time:*

The Last of the Soviets had a more profound effect on me. Alexievich says, 'I'm piecing together the history of "domestic", "interior" socialism. As it existed in a person's soul. I've always been drawn to this miniature expanse: one person, the individual. It's where everything happens.'

I had read Russian literature and journalism about the huge changes the country had gone through in the move from communism to capitalism. I had some idea, some understanding, of Russian experience. But reading these interviews with ordinary Russians in post-perestroika cities was like suddenly being introduced to the Russian psyche as a whole. I felt I'd never known who these people were before.

What struck me most particularly was how many people missed their lives under communism. We've been brought up to think that the privations of postwar Russia were unbearable – and in many cases they were – so it was odd to hear the children of parents who'd been sent to labour camps speak about regretting the loss of culture that came with the advent of capitalism. 'Our country was covered in banks and billboards.' 'An entire civilisation lies rotting on the trash heap.' One remembered that when the new work of a favourite poet was published, 'We'd queue round the block for a copy.'

I think sometimes about my friend Trevor, a writer whose twenty-year-old son has not read Camus and Sartre and Dostoevsky and Kafka, once the usual fare for thoughtful young men. I think about the time Trevor said to Corin that if he did not read fiction, he would be *a very lonely man.* This makes perfect sense to me, although it is probably wrong. Corin is most certainly not lonely; he has music, and his band, and the magazine he writes for. But I feel less lonely just thinking about Trevor saying that.

I've passed through my activist age, when it was my sworn duty to make sure every student I taught read at least one book. It's exhausting to be angry all the time. I try to remember what I learned years ago – that when the book became readily available in English households in the sixteenth and seventeenth centuries, people feared a kind of apocalypse of communication. Instead of sitting by the fire in the evening and talking, everyone would disappear into the silence of text, and civilisation would come to an end. Then there was the long-playing record, and then there was the radio, then the movies, and then, horror of horrors, the television. And now – well, here we are, still talking to each other.

Besides, when I look into the rooms of the two teenagers in my house they are happy reading, or texting, or checking their Instagram or listening to music, or, it seems, doing all of these things at once. I don't use any social media myself but I can feel the rich hum of theirs in our house. There are ways my two children are communicating, ways they are becoming themselves, that I don't intervene in – and that's as it should be.

*

But it used to be that when I stood in front of a class I felt an excited kinship, and a sense of my enormous luck – to be there, right then, amongst young people, as their reading and writing took shape. I still feel lucky, because it's a privilege to be next to young people at any stage of their lives. But sometimes, when I read their writing, I want to send up a howl of desolation. Their flimsy words scud across an empty landscape, a landscape unpopulated by all the books that came before. There's no weight, there's no texture, there's no echo, there's no depth. In the late '90s I used to chuckle to myself when I read the work of yet another young man whose style had been colonised by Cormac McCarthy or Tim Winton or Charles Bukowski. There's nothing to chuckle at anymore because my students haven't read any of these writers. There's no-one to be colonised by. Cue tumbleweeds.

I can't expect undergraduate students to have read as many books as I have – I am fifty and they are twenty – and not all can share this sense I have that literature is a conversation with history. That it can be turned to when we are seeking understanding of ourselves or our attitudes. That by examining it we can discover what kind of person we are, and how forces like capitalism, like communism, play a part in forming a person. That literature played its part in the invention of the teenager.

Nor do I expect my students to read *Stalky & Co*, or to channel Cormac McCarthy or Tim Winton or Charles Bukowski. I don't even expect them to have full command of their sentences when we first meet. Times have changed. These days I spend a good half of my class time demolishing and rebuilding sentences with my students, and the other half introducing them to as many works of literature as I can. I respect their right to be at university and I try to make sure they leave my classes having learned something, and – this comes second, and always must – having enjoyed themselves.

But oh, the silences in their writing. The rush of wind. The tumbleweeds.

Detail III

My old friend Patrick sent me a scan of a page torn out of an exercise book, scribbled on in a loose, fast-moving hand – the hand of someone speaking to themselves, barely seeing the page. It's written by David McComb, the lead singer of Western Australian band The Triffids, about their 1986 album *Born Sandy Devotional*. Patrick and my husband Russell and I spend some of our idle time making lists and sending them to each other. When Prince died we each made a list of our ten favourite Prince songs, and then Russell compiled them into a playlist (there were several overlaps, including 'Mountains' from *Parade* and 'The Ballad of Dorothy Parker' from *Sign o' the Times*). We also make lists of our favourite albums, of our heroes and heroines, our favourite books. It is a way of speaking to each other about a long shared history: the three of us have been together in one way or another for thirty or more years. Russell's favourite album is Prince's *Parade*; he has its barcode tattooed on his left bicep. Patrick has two favourites: *Parade* and *Liberty Belle and the Black Diamond Express*, The Go-Betweens' fourth album. My favourite album, of all time, without hesitation, is *Born Sandy Devotional*.

McComb writes:

the theme will be
Unrequited Love
But the language
will reach way above
and beyond that
VERY LITERARY to prevent it being soppy
Muscular, slow
droning long background strings
deft jazzy bass + drums

Why is it my favourite album? It is because it so willingly reaches for greatness. It is VERY LITERARY. But if Robert Forster of the Go-Betweens was Charlotte Brontë – more intellectual, more controlled – then David McComb was Emily, and *Born Sandy Devotional* his *Wuthering Heights*, a masterpiece both helpless and willed. The Triffids wrote landscapes of sound, grand songs to accommodate the grand feelings and deep, commanding vocals of its lead singer. They made a kind of operatic beauty out of simple things. They were prepared to find Western Australia – Perth, no less – a place of great passions. *Born Sandy Devotional*, with its mad, apparently meaningless title, says *yes* to art.

I remember where I was when I learned that David McComb had died, just before his thirty-seventh birthday. He'd had a heart transplant a few years earlier, having ruined his cardiovascular system with excessive drinking and drug taking. Finally the heart rejected him, or he it. Another note, this from McComb's London diaries, counts beers drunk on an ordinary night out: 'Personally, it was definitely a "light" night as far as imbibing goes: nine or eleven pints, which is practically technically a "night off", "a night on the wagon" per se.' Despite the emerging narrative of disaster, I love this sentence: its sprouting ugliness, all those self-conscious quotation marks. I love that pompous 'per se', which is only there for the sound of it. I love the showing off, the self-dramatising, the youthful use of words like 'imbibing'. I love the sound of 'practically technically', like dice cracking together. The Triffids, and David McComb in particular, taught me that writing like this – being grandiose, showing off, indulging the self – wasn't a crime. Or it wasn't if through the practice of it you could produce art.

Annie Dillard says:

One of the things I know about writing is this: spend it all, shoot it, play it, lose it, all, right away, every time . . . These things fill from behind, from beneath, like well water . . . Anything you do not give freely and abundantly becomes lost to you.

It was 1999 and I was driving somewhere in the dark, most likely to or from Sydney, from or to the Blue Mountains. The radio played 'Wide Open Road' from *Born Sandy Devotional*. Tears coursed down my face. I felt the odd, displaced grief of losing someone you never knew: grief for McComb's loneliness, his or all of ours in the face of death. And grief because I had never had the chance to say to him, Music like yours allows art in others. It is a part of who I am, and because of that David McComb still lives.

In *Moby-Dick*, Herman Melville writes: 'Out of the trunk, the branches grow; out of them, the twigs. So, in productive subjects, grow the chapters.'

It took me a long time to come to *Moby-Dick*. I'd thought it would be a heavy tale of adventure, of men with fierce brows ploughing through wild seas. I thought the whole book would be this, just the ceaseless, male pursuit of a lumbering metaphor. There are plenty of fierce brows, as it turns out, and some wild seas, but there is also this:

Steering north-eastward from the Crozetts, we fell in with vast meadows of brit, the minute, yellow substance, upon which the Right Whale largely feeds. For leagues and leagues it undulated round us, so that we seemed to be sailing through boundless fields of ripe and golden wheat.

On the second day, numbers of Right Whales were seen, who, secure from the attach of a Sperm Whaler like the Pequod, with open jaws swam sluggishly through the brit, which, adhering to the fringing fibres of that wondrous Venetian blind in their mouths, was in that manner separated from the water that escaped at the lip.

As morning mowers, who side by side slowly and seethingly advance their scythes through the long wet grass of marshy means; even so these monsters swam, making strange, grassy, cutting sounds; and leaving behind them endless swaths of blue upon the yellow sea.

Herman Melville was reading the works of Shakespeare for the first time when he wrote *Moby-Dick*, and these passages demonstrate that. My mother used to say that what she loved best about Shakespeare was that he didn't care about mixing his metaphors; he took arms against a sea of troubles. In *Moby-Dick* Melville was the same. He piled idea on idea, image on image; he reached into himself and threw out loop after loop of a seemingly never-ending rope of thought. It is distracting, sometimes – that venetian blind makes me forget the central image in these paragraphs: the *mowers*. Whales passing, mouths open, through paddocks of brit, or krill, cutting it down, mowing it. One is also distracted by the alliteration: the fringing fibres, side by side, slowly and seethingly, the marshy means. But what riches of language dwell here.

James Wood says we should not pity Melville, even though his masterpiece was initially met with almost total silence, 'for in writing *Moby-Dick*, Melville wrote the novel that is every writer's dream of freedom. It is as though he painted a patch of sky for the imprisoned.' In using words – so *many* of them – Melville scorned temperance. He spent it all, lost it all, right away. We should not think of what it must have been to write what he surely knew was his greatest book and to hear almost nothing back.

Born Sandy Devotional was widely praised, although the critical success of The Triffids never did translate into significant international fame or serious money. But McComb, too, was painting his patch of sky. Any artist lucky enough to be doing their best work will tell you that the work is enough.

Patrick once told me that autumn awakened in him a feeling of 'satisfied melancholy'. As I write, it is February in Katoomba, February following an intolerable January, the hottest Australia has ever had. When I came out into the living room this morning I noticed that the angle of the light had changed. The cat sat in its pour, eyes happily closed. The days now have that thread of cool in them, a call, a reminder, of what soon will be. Having moved, the light will begin to age, yellowing like leaves. The leaves themselves will begin to turn. Satisfied melancholy approaches.

I made friends with Patrick for several reasons. First, he was just so beautiful. Tall, with unruly, curling golden hair and pale blue eyes. Unshaven, regular-featured. Russell and I have often remarked that a surprising number of famous people look like Patrick: most of all Michael Hutchence, but also, oddly, Prince and, well, David McComb. I was not the only young woman to swim into the disintegrating net of Patrick's heterosexuality.

I liked him also because he made me laugh. When a friend and I wrote a series of comic poems about an imaginary Beat poet for our university radio show, we asked him to perform them. He threw himself into that performance with such abandon that I laughed until I was shrieking,

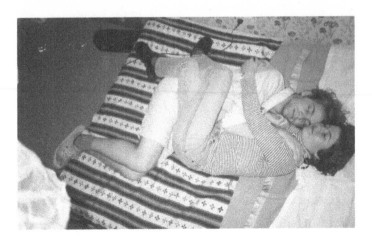

had to slam out of the sound booth and fall on my knees, crying, howling. But we first made friends by talking about reading. Patrick read like a girl, and like a very particular kind of girl; he had read books that I thought only I had read. Committed outsiders, we used to walk around the headland near my North Bondi share house and talk and talk about books. A lyric from one of the songs Patrick and Russell wrote together: 'I like you, you remind me of me.'

If *Moby-Dick* is anything, it is the book or books that Melville could not help writing on his way to writing it. The trunk of plot grows branches, and then twigs, in profusion. Chapters of adventure are interrupted for other chapters – an ocean of chapters – of digression. The digression sometimes takes the form of disquisition on some part or another of the whale – a chapter for his whiteness, more chapters for the weapons used to catch and kill him, a chapter on the spout, a chapter on the tail. To wit: 'Five great motions are peculiar to it. First, when used as a fin for progression; Second, when used as a mace in battle; Third, in sweeping; Fourth, in lobtailing; Fifth, in peaking flukes.'

Sometimes *Moby-Dick*'s narrator, Ishmael, leaves his narrator's body altogether and becomes omniscient, entering (in an impossible third person) into the captain's cabin, or disporting with the second mate, Stubb, or his superior, Starbuck, on the bulwarks. Some chapters race through the waters alongside a whale about to be caught and killed. Sometimes the reader has water dashed full in their face. Some chapters come to a complete halt while they comb through other writings, other texts on the Leviathan. But my favourite chapters of all, the reason I was finally able to read the book, are the chapters about friendship – about the meeting of Ishmael and Queequeg, a South Sea harpooneer, at the Spouter-Inn in New Bedford.

The inn is full, and Ishmael can only stay if he shares not just a room but a bed with Queequeg, a stranger. Ishmael is first to bed, where he lies watching Queequeg prepare to turn in next to him. He is angry, suspicious of Queequeg as he performs a little ritual of prayer with a small wooden idol, and believes he will not sleep a wink. Queequeg climbs into bed and there begin the most delightful physical negotiations, opening in disgust and repulsion, and ending in amity, the two sleeping as soundly as they have ever slept. 'Upon waking next morning about daylight, I found Queequeg's arm thrown over me in the most loving and affectionate manner. You had almost thought I had been his wife.' Here is *Moby-Dick's* most intimate relationship, a tender, affectionate friendship which endures until – well, perhaps you have to read the book. But it is Ishmael and Queequeg who keep the story alive and warm. It takes some time for Ishmael to rouse Queequeg sufficiently, to remove the arm that is holding him so lovingly to the bed. The long meditation of Ishmael on that arm teaches us to pay attention, teaches us to love Queequeg as Ishmael does. Teaches us to love life, as Melville does. To pay attention to its beautiful multiplicity.

When my mother died, various odd, almost physical changes took place in me. One was a very distinct feeling that my life was like a photograph album, and that someone was going back to its beginning and removing all the images of my mother and me. This felt as real in my body as though it was actually happening, sections of my life dematerialising as I walked around, as I worked, as I looked out of the kitchen window at night.

I've just understood where this sensation came from, why its seed lay dormant in my body. In *The Voyage of the Dawn Treader*, the fifth book in the Narnia series, Lucy must read a magician's book to undo a spell. As she reads the spell aloud, alone in a dark room in an apparently empty house,

> the colours came into the capital letters at the top of the page and the pictures began appearing in the margins. It was like when you hold to the fire something written in Invisible Ink and the writing gradually shows up . . .

This, in reverse. All the images of my mother – standing beside me, holding me, drawing with me, reading with me – disappearing from the page. Strange, to think that a death might make one feel robbed of the one real thing that is left, besides ashes or a body: memory.

Then, after a year, two years, the photograph album began to fill up again, as though invisible ink had been held to the fire. This happened at the same time as I began to feel that I could read books once more. My mother gave me a copy of *Moby-Dick* when I was fifteen or sixteen: every year, she gave us each a pile of books and then greedily waited for the conversation that would arise once we had read them. I didn't read it then, but I have read it now, and here she is. I hear her voice.

Patrick and I were flatmates when he fell in love with his partner Yianni; months later I fell in love with Patrick's friend Russell. Patrick and Russell and Yianni and I send each other old photographs, along with the lists. Autumn it most certainly is: we are all, now, in our fifties. One of us will die first. For a while, that person will disappear. But with the passing of time, under the spell of art, we are restored. The songs still played, the books still read, the pictures visible once more. Look: it's 1996 and there we are, the four of us, posing for the camera, drunk on sex and new love and friendship. Our eyes alight. Our limbs entwined.

Photographs

Permissions

Every effort has been made to contact copyright holders and obtain permission to reproduce material as relevant. The publisher welcomes any information or enquiry in this regard.

The publishers wish to acknowledge the following copyright holders for kind permission to reproduce material in this book:

Collins, Suzanne, extract from *The Hunger Games*, Scholastic, New York, 2008. Reproduced by kind permission of Scholastic, Inc.

Dillard, Annie, extract from *The Writing Life*, Harper and Row, New York, 1989. Reproduced by kind permission of Russell and Volkening.

The Details

Garner, Helen, extracts from *Monkey Grip*, McPhee Gribble, Melbourne, 1977, and *The Children's Bach*, McPhee Gribble, Melbourne, 1984. Reproduced by kind permission of the author.

Hogan, Ron, extract from interview with George Saunders, 2000, http://www.beatrice.com/wordpress/. Reproduced by kind permission of Ron Hogan.

McComb, David, extract from *Tour Diaries 1989*, and note on *Born Sandy Devotional*, http://www.thetriffids.com. Reproduced by kind permission of Graham Lee.

Murray, Les, extract from *Dog Fox Field*, Carcanet Press, Manchester, 1991. Reproduced by kind permission of the Estate of Les Murray c/o Margaret Connolly & Associates Pty Ltd.

Stow, Randolph, extract from *The Merry-Go-Round in the Sea*, Macdonald, London, 1965. Reproduced by kind permission of Sheil Land Associates.

The Paris Review, extracts from interviews with Truman Capote (The Art of Fiction No. 17) and S.J. Perelman (The Art of Fiction No. 31). Reproduced by kind permission of the Wylie Agency.

Acknowledgements

To Vicki Hastrich, Lucinda Holdforth and Charlotte Wood.

To Russell Daylight, Alice Daylight, Patrick Daylight.

Thanks also to Ben Ball, Joss Bennett, Kerry Bennett, Pippita Bennett, Jemma Birrell, Siobhán Cantrill, Jenny Darling, Clara Finlay, Ashley Hay, James Ley, Patrick McIntyre, Catriona Menzies-Pike, John O'Carroll, Stephen Romei, Meredith Rose, Geordie Williamson, Vikki Willmott-Sharp, Tim Winton, and my students, every one of them.

Some of the essays in this collection were previously published as follows: 'Detail I' (as 'Learning to See' in *Island* magazine (ed. Geordie Williamson); 'Vagina' in *Best Australian Essays 2016* (Black Inc., ed. Geordie Williamson); 'The Difficulty is the Point' in *The Guardian*; 'Just Anguish' as a talk called 'S.J. Perelman: The Writer Who Changed Me' for the Sydney Writers' Festival, 2016; 'The Worst that Could Happen' in *Sydney Review of Books* (ed. James Ley); versions of 'Georgia Blain' in the *Sydney Morning Herald*, the *Age*, and on the Stella Prize website; 'A Mole, a Viper, a Toad' in *Sydney Review of Books* (ed. Catriona Menzies-Pike); and 'Inventing the Teenager' (as 'Keeping Faith with Words') in *Griffith Review* (ed. Ashley Hay).

The writing of this book was generously supported by the Australia Council for the Arts.

About the author

Tegan Bennett Daylight is a writer, teacher and critic. Her books include the Stella Award shortlisted *Six Bedrooms* and the novels *Safety* and *Bombora*. She lives in the Blue Mountains with her husband and two children.